GREAT GOD OF WONDERS

*The Life of Grace and
the Hope of Glory*

D1406422

Maurice Roberts

THE BANNER OF TRUTH TRUST

THE BANNER OF TRUTH TRUST
3 Murrayfield Road, Edinburgh EH12 6EL
PO Box 621, Carlisle, PA 17013, USA

*

© Maurice Roberts 2003
ISBN 0 85151 837 0

*

Typeset in 11.5/14 pt Adobe Garamond at
the Banner of Truth Trust, Edinburgh
Printed and bound in Great Britain by
Creative Print & Design (Wales),
Ebbw Vale

Contents

Publisher's Preface   vii

THE LIFE OF GRACE

Prayer

1	On Seeking God	3
2	Getting Started in Prayer	10
3	Secret Prayer Openly Rewarded	19

Living for God

4	Godliness	29
5	Union and Communion with Christ	37
6	No Mere Memory	43
7	Living with Our Limitations	50
8	'No Cross, No Crown'	56
9	The Strife of Tongues	62

The Fellowship of the Church

10	The Duty of Mutual Submission	71
11	Dealing with Our Differences	78
12	The Minister's Wife	87
13	'In the Time of Old Age'	93
14	Why Christians Must Be Readers	101

Delighting in the Character of God

15	'Great God of Wonders'	111
16	God of Righteousness	118
17	The 'Slowness' of God's Ways	124
18	God's Secrets – the Believer's Comforts	132
19	The Gentleness of Christ	139
20	No Greater Love	145

Understanding God's Truth

21	'I Am the Truth'	155
22	Justification: An Imperilled Doctrine	162
23	'The Spirits in Prison'	172
24	The History of Unbelief	182

THE HOPE OF GLORY
The Second Coming and Heaven

25	The Believer's Half-Life	191
26	Entering into Rest	198
27	Heaven, Resurrection, and the Coming Glory	204
28	'As the Lightning . . .'	213
29	From Prophecy to History	220
30	Thy Kingdom Come	226

Publisher's Preface

L ike both the earlier titles by the same author, *The Thought of God* (ISBN 0 85151 658 0, 256 pp., pbk, 1993), and *The Christian's High Calling* (ISBN 0 85151 792 7, 240 pp., pbk., 2000), this book consists of articles which originally appeared as editorials in *The Banner of Truth*, the magazine which Maurice Roberts edited between January 1988 and January 2003. Each chapter is self-contained and very helpful for devotional reading and meditation. Readers who have already appreciated the articles as they appeared each month will wish to have them in this convenient and permanent form, while those who come to them for the first time will find them warmly biblical, pastoral, inspiring and thought-provoking.

Reviewers of the earlier books have found in them both a heart-searching diagnosis of contemporary ills and a comforting application of the biblical cure. One reader observed of *The Christian's High Calling*: 'Any Christian who wishes to be gently drawn above and beyond the rising tide of superficial Christian literature will be richly rewarded by reading this book.'

Maurice Roberts' focus is never man-centred. His emphasis is always on God in his majesty, the 'great God of wonders' revealed in Scripture, 'the God of all grace, who hath called us unto his eternal glory by Christ Jesus'. As Roberts points out, 'To think about God aright is the most exciting occupation possible for any created being.' It is also vitally important, since 'all men become like the objects of their worship'. In answer to the question, how can Christians today exert a greater influence for God and for righteousness, Roberts suggests, 'We might begin by acquainting ourselves better with the God of righteousness himself, and then beseech him to stretch out his mighty arm again.'

The Publisher
March 2003

THE LIFE OF GRACE
– PRAYER

I

On Seeking God

Whatever the pressures are to the contrary, the serious Christian *must* keep a careful watch over the inner state and attitude of his own soul. Just as there are temptations for the careless and the idle Christian, so too are there snares for the Christian who becomes too busy. We are too busy whenever we cannot safeguard our times of private prayer, meditation and devotional Bible reading. What happens when outward duties become excessive and over-demanding is that inner, secret duties are performed in a merely routine way. It is all too possible to conduct our private and family worship with our minds half taken up with other things. We persuade ourselves that we have been worshipping God, but on such occasions we have been no better than those to whom God said, 'This people draweth nigh unto me with their mouth, and honoureth me with their lips; but their heart is far from me' (*Matt*. 15:8).

The tendency of our soul when we allow ourselves to pray, read and worship with only half our minds is that we become accustomed to it. 'Practice makes perfect' in bad habits as well as in good ones. Days go by when we attend to the familiar work of secret worship in our 'closet' and yet never really put our heart in what we are doing. The sacred page is turned, but the lofty truths which we are reading have no effect upon our minds or upon our characters. This bad practice, if indulged in for long, becomes the norm. Days become weeks and weeks become months, during which we unconsciously slip deeper and deeper into the practice of prayerless praying and shallow, unfeeling devotions. For this soul sleep there is a high price to pay.

How do we account for the fact that scores and hundreds of persons who once called themselves 'evangelical' and even 'Reformed' have over the years slipped from this early zeal for God into an easy conformity? Their once burning concern to defend and promote the truth of God has in too many cases become no more than a comfortable acceptance of the prevailing apathy. No doubt there is in us all a youthful exuberance which requires curbing and maturing with the experience gained as we grow in knowledge. But if growth in knowledge results in loss of conviction, loss of zeal for truth, loss of passion for the distinctives of the gospel and a willingness to associate with the enemies of the truth, we have paid too high a price for our 'knowledge'. Something has been forgotten. The excellence of true religion is that it exerts a *power* over our heart and over our entire life. This power is the spiritual influence of grace and truth acting on every part of our souls and firing us with a conscientious desire to advance God's honour with all our might in this world as long as we live. When we cease to live realistically for God, commending truth fervently and combatting error unflinchingly, we betray the fact that the power of God has declined in our life. We can still repeat the formulas of orthodoxy, perhaps, and we can still say what is sound and scriptural. But there is not the same passion or conviction in what we say. It is sadly all too clear that although in such cases we retain a 'form of godliness', we have 'denied the power thereof' (*2 Tim.* 3:5).

The remedy for all such lukewarmness is to 'repent and do the first works' (*Rev.* 2:5). That is, we must put first the state and condition of our own soul. There is no known way to do this which does not involve us in heartfelt repentance, evangelical sorrow and renewed attention to the secret place. To keep up the power of godliness in the soul is about the most difficult thing the Christian can do. A violin hung up on the wall soon goes out of tune, and a knife in constant use quickly loses its sharpness. So does the soul, because of indwelling sin, soon lose its spiritual 'edge' and become untuned for communion with God and other spiritual exercises. When this happens, the Christian can go through the motions of prayer, worship and service to God, but there is a difference which cannot fail to be noticed – by others as well as by ourselves.

Too many prayers and sermons which we pray and preach betray the neglect of communion with God in private. The vehicle of devotion still travels along, but it is obvious that the tyres are flat and the whole machine in need of overhaul. It must surely be agreed by all serious Christians that the ideal state of soul is that in which we have a *conscious* delight in God and are emotionally involved in all that we say to him in prayer and praise. All Christians know what it is at times to *enjoy* God's presence, to be 'filled' to the point at which we feel the whole world to be one vast nothing by comparison with having God. At such seasons of blessing a believer 'rides on the high places of the earth' (*Deut.* 32: 13) and soars aloft on eagle's wings. Such times are high points in his experience and they assure us of the truth of the gospel better than a dozen manuals on apologetics could do. To have such seasons of spiritual unction when we feed on the heavenly manna and sit consciously under Christ's shadow is to know that true religion is more by far than notion. At such times we 'have the witness in ourselves' that God is true and that Christianity is the religion of heaven.

On the other hand, the Christian knows what it is to go through periods of spiritual sluggishness and deadness. At such times prayer is agonizingly difficult and the actions of the soul feel wooden. This night-time of the soul is a joyless time for those who profess that 'for them to live is Christ' (*Phil.* 1:21). Nevertheless, there is even then in the Christian's experience a 'lesser light to rule the night'. This is the activity of a Christian's conscience telling him that he must arise and stir himself up to seek the face of God anew. The hypocrite is happy to sleep on at his ease. But the believer has conscientious stirrings of heart which rouse him sooner or later out of his slumbering state like the cockerel which electrified Peter's soul and drew from him hot tears of self-loathing.

All the troubles in the church are related, more or less, to our failure to watch over our souls. It is in our twilight states and 'midnight' moods that we are most likely to speak the foolish word, voice the hurtful criticism or make the hasty decision. Such things are said and done in a moment, but the harm which follows may last a lifetime. Who is there that would not wish a thousand times to re-live a thoughtless moment or re-word a thoughtless statement, if only he could? Had we but walked more closely with Christ, had we but spent longer in his sanctifying presence before these sad moments in life, we might well not need now to bear the scars of regret upon our memory and upon our conscience! But we had learnt to be self-confident and to suppose ourselves strong. God therefore left us to ourselves, that we might know what is in our hearts.

The way to measure whether we are lively or else formal in our devotions is to face up to the question: are we *seeking* God in them or not? To *seek* God is to desire him, to want him, to thirst for him above all else. This must be done, as Christ teaches by word and example, in some solitary place alone and with the 'door shut'. The way to get God's blessing is to put ourselves down low in the dust before him. The more we prostrate our soul before him, the more likely we are to get a fresh taste of his love and grace, for God gives 'grace to the humble' (*James* 4:6). To get a blessing from our Bible is similarly done when once we are able to 'tremble at his word' (*Isa.* 66:2). On the other hand, if we approach God and his Word with little or no self-abasement, we shall be sent away empty and unblessed.

There is a world of difference between the way one person approaches the means of grace and the way another does. This point is clearly made by our Lord in his parable of the Pharisee and the publican (*Luke* 18:10f). We are, however, not always inclined to come to God with the publican's shame-facedness and self-abasement. Unwisely, we grow too familiar with God and, all unconsciously, talk over-confidently to him, forgetting that even Christ himself, who at times prayed 'with strong crying and tears', was 'heard in that he *feared*' (*Heb.* 5:7).

Our best examples of Christian spirituality in past days often made 'rules' for themselves to help them avoid formalism and to promote the power of godliness in their own souls. Jonathan Edwards did so. So did M'Cheyne. Are there any 'rules' which a believer might use to assist him in this lifelong task of living and worshipping in the conscious enjoyment of God? We suggest that the following guidelines should be borne in mind by Christians who seriously wish to live in a lively state of soul:

1. There are different kinds of prayer which we are called on to pray. Each day we are to bear up to God our family, our church, our nation and its concerns, missionaries far and near, and the cause of Christ in general. However, we ought to have also another kind of prayer in which we are not so much praying for others as wrestling to get our souls close to God. This latter type of praying is what has probably fallen most into abeyance in our own day. But it is essential that we *seek* God's face for his own sake and desire him because he is God, the fountain of all spiritual life and joy. He is the life of our soul.

2. It is a mistake habitually to leave off praying before we have been *moved*. Our expectation should be that as we abase ourselves before God he will warm our hearts with gladness. This is a part of the 'lifting up of the downcast' by which 'out of weakness we are made strong' (*Heb.* 11:34). It is good

for us in secret prayer to be moved to tears, either of joy or of repentance. At any rate, there is something to be *felt* in prayer, and it is to our loss if we rise and go before we have felt anything. Similarly with our Bible reading, it is good when we feel our hearts burning within us by the time we have finished. We may not always have this experience, but we sometimes do, and it is right to feel disappointed when we leave the throne of grace unmoved. If we expect to feel nothing, we shall probably receive nothing. But never to feel anything when we pray and worship God is a loss to *us*.

2

Getting Started in Prayer[1]

The subject before us relates to problems which we encounter in prayer. What do we really mean by prayer? The definition which we should be familiar with is that given by the *Westminster Shorter Catechism*. It is worth committing to memory: 'Prayer is an offering up of our desires unto God, for things agreeable to his will, in the name of Christ, with confession of our sins and thankful acknowledgement of his mercies.'

We may divide the theme of prayer into two parts: *secret prayer* and *public prayer*. Secret prayer refers necessarily to what we do on our own, when there is nobody to listen but God. Public prayer refers, of course, to what we do when we gather in a prayer meeting. One of the Christians engages in prayer and leads us to the throne of grace. We must be more circumspect in spoken prayer in a meeting than we need be in secret and alone with God.

Prayer is the natural response of a converted heart to an inner desire for communion with God. In a sense there ought not to be any problems. However, when we come down to the details of how to pray, whether it be in secret

[1] From a lecture on *The Difficulties of Prayer*.

or in public, everyone becomes acquainted with some of these difficulties.

I take it for granted that we are agreed that *all* of us ought to pray. We are surely agreed that we may pray sitting, standing or walking about; that we ought to be praying without ceasing. Whenever we have an odd moment throughout the day when our minds are not taken up, we can send up an arrow prayer to God. I am going to concentrate this evening on problems that we find in certain areas of the duty of prayer.

First of all there is the problem of getting started in prayer, and getting organized in our own private lives in prayer. Now you will see what I mean by that. If we never have a special time for prayer throughout the day, and if we never organize our time so that we have at least a time of prayer in every day, then in a sense you could say that we are *never* praying. It is not enough that we should simply be praying here and there in odd moments as we walk about and go about our duties in life. We should be doing that, but we should also have stated and set times for private devotion and prayer.

Another problem is this: the tension that arises in our secret prayers between the *form* of prayer and the *spirit* of prayer.

Still another difficulty is this, that everybody sooner or later finds in prayer the tendency to weariness. That is the state of mind in which from time to time even the best of men and women who pray are tempted to think to themselves, 'I'm so weary of prayer: must I go on and on?'

So, then, there is the problem of getting started in prayer, and getting our own lives organized with a view to having secret prayer. We all know that the Christian desires to pray. Even those who are not Christians have an instinctive desire to pray. Prayer is one of the things which marks out a man from a beast. It is instinctive in man to cry out to God. I shall not take up further time with this point, but even atheists have been known to pray in times of trouble. Worldly persons say when things go wrong, 'Oh, let's pray that it will work out.' They never go to God's house, but that is their attitude. However, although the Christian especially desires to pray, he often feels that it is difficult to organize himself to pray and it is often very difficult to get started, to get into the spirit of prayer. Some days it is easy: some days it is very hard. We should have method in our lives. Let us try to be practical.

Every one of us should have a place in our own homes – or wherever it is – where we know we can go to pray. If we do not have a place to get alone with God, it is very difficult to pray. It is intensely difficult to devote the whole of your life to concentration upon this duty of seeking the face of God, if we do not have the privacy of a place where we can meet alone with God. Normally, of course, it will be our own bedroom. Some are privileged to have a study or a room in the house where they will not be disturbed. Also a time must be made as well.

We need a time each day in which we can go to be alone with God. Obviously there are variations permissible here. The ideal would be in the morning, before we begin the duties of the day. However, it may be that in certain cases, for various reasons that just is not possible. It would not be wise for instance for a young mother to be on her knees praying when she should be preparing the breakfast. So times will vary, but we need to have a time in the day when we are as awake as can be.

People ask, 'How long should I pray for?' This depends on the individual. I would give you this general rule: try to pray yourself 'out'. Try to make sure that you have prayed everything you want to say to God. Empty the vessel of your heart out fully to God. Try to make sure, if you can, that you have said everything you desire to say. This may take about half an hour, less or more. Half an hour is perhaps the sort of time many will give daily to prayer in our busy generation. Try to have enough time to pray to God without being hurried.

You need to be able to concentrate. You need to be warm. There is no good praying if you are in a cold bedroom. Otherwise all the time you are on your knees you will be mentally switching on an electric fire! Be practical. You need to be in the very best state of body and mind.

Then try to shut the whole world out. I recommend praying on one's knees. Of course, there are times when that might be inappropriate, but I think that ought to be the general rule. Shut yourself in. Be on your own with God.

How do you get started? I recommend that we read from the Bible first, and that we read with a view to preparing our hearts for fellowship with God in prayer. For instance, you might read Psalm 1, and having read it and thought about its meaning, you then go on your knees and pray something like this: 'O Lord, give me the blessedness of the man who does not sit in the seat of the scornful or walk in the ways of the ungodly, and this and that. But rather Lord, give me the spirit of the man who is planted as a tree beside the water courses: the blessing of the man who is not driven about like chaff in the streets. Give me, Lord, the character of the man who will stand in the day of judgment, when the wicked shall be overthrown and destroyed.' Now, I believe that is the right way to learn to pray. M'Cheyne and other writers on the subject tell us that. Take your Bible, read a passage, then turn what you have read into prayer. Do not do it mechanically. Turn everything that you can remember into prayer. Pray that God would give to you the spirit of prayer.

Next, should we pray aloud or should we pray silently? I would recommend that you do both on different occasions, depending upon the state of your own soul and of your own mind. What are we aiming at in secret prayer? I would say what we are aiming at, above all else, is to bring our hearts to God in such a way that we hide nothing from him. We wish to be able to get up from our knees and feel in our consciences that we have exposed ourselves in every way to God. We have laid our very hearts bare before his gaze.

I come now to the problem of the form and the spirit in prayer. And I must explain to you first of all what I mean. It is possible to buy 'prayer books', books which actually write out prayers word for word. Most famous of all is the *Book of Common Prayer*, which has long been in use in the Church of England. Are we to use books of prayer? Are we to commit prayers to memory, and then repeat them, rather like the Lord's Prayer? Or, are we to make up our own prayers? Protestant churches have normally believed and taught that we should depend on God to teach us how to pray. We learn to pray by reading and also through the influence of the Holy Spirit.

Books of prayer are not absolutely wrong. I do not think anyone would ever want to go that far. But what you and I need to learn to do is to have real heart-to-heart communion with God, because, after all, that is what prayer is. It is the pouring out of our hearts to God. We must believe, first of all, that the Bible is the perfect book of prayer, just as it is the perfect book of doctrine. This is especially so of the Psalms, which are given to teach us how to frame our words in prayer to God. But the whole Bible, and especially the Lord's Prayer, is a manual of instruction on how to pray.

That is one aspect of the subject. It is the *form*. Then there is the other aspect, that of the *spirit* of prayer. These two must be kept in view by us. We should endeavour, I believe, to pray to God with a certain form in our prayers. I mean we should endeavour to pray in an orderly sort of manner, in a logical sort of manner. This is illustrated by the Lord's Prayer. The Lord's Prayer has order and form. It is not haphazard.

The order here is this: We begin with the glory of God; the Kingdom of God; the will of God. Everything begins with God: his glory, his kingdom, his will. And then we descend to ourselves: our needs, our sins, our problems. That is what I mean by order in prayer. We should endeavour to teach ourselves to pray with an orderliness and methodicalness of mind. It is a biblical practice and it is a biblical thing to do.

But then, too, orderliness can be as cold as an icicle. You can have the most perfect prayer in beautiful English (the 'Queen's English', as we say), and it can be full of poetical phrases and lovely liturgical sentences, but it can be, as I say, as cold as ice. What we need therefore is to have also the fire of the Spirit of God within us. One of the first things which I think a Christian learns when on his knees is that in prayer God helps him. It can be so difficult to begin. But what you discover is, that as you start to pray with stammering words, you suddenly feel the ice in your heart melting. You do not know how it works but words come, because thoughts come, and emotions come, and you begin to warm to the theme. Whereas you began cold and with inertia in your soul, before long you are like a blacksmith, hammering at the anvil, as hard as you can go. The 'sparks' are now flying. Now the Spirit of God is the One who inspires prayer, and this, I do not hesitate to say, is what Paul means when he says to us, 'We do not know what to pray for as we ought, but the Spirit maketh intercession for us with groanings that cannot be uttered' (*Rom.* 8:26).

That is to say that the Holy Spirit teaches us how to pray. He does not intercede as Christ does. Christ intercedes for us at the right hand of God, apart from us and outside us. But the Holy Spirit intercedes within us. The Holy Spirit is the Spirit of prayer. However, having said that, we must go on to add that God is sovereign in the gift of prayer, and he gives more of a gift of prayer to some Christians than to others. This is true in every congregation. Immediately you can think of some who have a gift of prayer that is quite exceptional, but others have a gift of prayer which is perhaps no more than ordinary.

But every one of us should stir up the gift within him and endeavour to become stronger in prayer. It is a wonderful thing when a congregation begins to be full of mighty wrestlers in prayer.

One word about prayer 'lists'. I do not want in any sense to be disparaging when I say this. Of course we have to remind ourselves, by one means or another, of certain things and persons to pray for. That is inevitable; we have to do that. But when you have your list of things that you are going to pray for – persons, and various places – put the list down and then depend upon God to illuminate your mind. I do not think it is a wise practice to be tied to a list, as though we have to mention every detail of every point in that list necessarily. I say this because God gives to his people in prayer what we call 'access' and 'liberty'.

Let me say a word about those two things. They are really the same thing. Our forefathers were right to say that this is a most vital aspect of prayer. This is perhaps the pinnacle of prayer.

Nine times out of ten we pray and we find it very difficult to 'get through'. We have plenty of words, but do you know what I mean when I say that you pray and you still feel 'wooden'? You will know this experience. But we must never be content with that. What we should strive for is to 'get through', to get 'access' to God.

That is the most blessed experience, in my opinion, of any experience you can have upon earth. It is the nearest thing to being in glory, to have this 'access' to God. It melts the soul and the heart of the person who has it. He can be quite literally bathed in tears of joy. Now that should be a commonplace experience for the people of God. It is a mistake in prayer to go on our knees, and stop after ten minutes because we think that we have not 'got through'. We have been praying correctly, we have been praying with the right form, and with plenty of words, but now we say, 'O, I have not *felt* very much'. So we stop praying.

Do not get off your knees too quickly. Pray on, because you know the experience that Jacob had with the angel was this: he wrestled till he prevailed. He said, 'I will not let thee go except thou bless me' (*Gen.* 32:26).

We ought to have that vision. We ought not always to go from the place of prayer until we have *felt* the dew coming down from heaven upon our spirits. That is what is referred to in Psalm 133: the dew that comes from heaven upon the hills of Zion, that anointing on the head of Aaron which flowed down the garments and skirts of his robe. That is what we should regard as a thing to strive for in prayer. We will not always get it. But every so often we *shall* feel this presence of God in prayer.

3

Secret Prayer Openly Rewarded

When God was about to bless his people with their long-promised Messiah, he raised up Simeon and Anna to pray 'with all prayer and supplication', night and day. God's 'secret is with them that fear him' (*Psa.* 25:14). These two were among a remnant in Israel who 'looked for redemption in Jerusalem' (*Luke* 2:38). They have a very honourable place in God's Word and deserve to be remembered affectionately. What do we know about them?

Of Simeon we read that he was 'just and devout' (*Luke* 2:25). His profession of godliness was not feigned or Pharisaic but real and true. In a very dark and dreary age this man had a genuine knowledge of God. He is a reminder to us that Christ has his jewels even in the worst of times. Simeon was a man who, by grace, rose above the gloom of his day and shone in the eye of God as a man of faith and hope. The grey mediocrity of those times did not drown his soul in unbelief or poison his spirit with cynicism. Though what he saw in God's house must have grieved him sorely, he devoted himself to a ministry which no eye of man saw. He prayed, hoped and longed for a better day to dawn. And he did not hope in vain.

It is stated of Simeon that he was 'waiting for the consolation of Israel' (*Luke* 2:25). He did not form a party to agitate for political or religious reform. Rather, he set himself to wait on God to break into the affairs of the nation again. He believed God's faithfulness to the ancient promises of a coming Saviour. We do not know how long he had been waiting but it must have been for many years before we see him here on the page of sacred Scripture in the one place of God's Word where he is mentioned. He is a bright example to us of the virtue of patient waiting on the Lord and persistent expectation.

To sustain his faith Simeon was also given a divine promise: 'It was revealed unto him by the Holy Ghost that he should not see death, before he had seen the Lord's Christ' (*Luke* 2:26). Just how this promise was revealed to him we may not know, whether through an inspired man living in his earlier life-time, or by an inner voice revealing to him this divine privilege immediately in his mind. However the message came to Simeon, he was not unfaithful to the heavenly vision but was strong in faith and in the expectation of its fulfilment to the very last. This sublime secret was the hidden source of his spiritual strength, the assurance that he would with his very eyes see for himself the Messiah and Saviour of the world.

There is little or no prayer in our souls until we have a vision of what God may do in this world, and even in our own lifetime. Faith must be constantly fuelled and re-fuelled by the promises of God. Where there is no such expectation of getting good in this life from the hand of God our faith sinks into a state of sleep. Prayer falls till it is a mere formality.

Of Anna, we know that she was a widow of great age, having lost her husband after only seven years of marriage. Her family descended from the tribe of Asher and her father's name was Phanuel. She is described as 'a prophetess' (*Luke* 2:36), a remarkable fact in view of the cessation of the Writing Prophets some four hundred years earlier, Malachi being the last. We assume that her prophetic gift, or rather the Holy Spirit, had enabled her, like Simeon, to know that the birth of the glorious Saviour was close at hand. She had consecrated almost her entire life to fasting and prayer 'night and day'. It is clear however that there existed in Jerusalem a number of others, not named in Scripture, who at this time were longing for God to revive his work in the church.

The picture we have, then, in this short passage of Scripture is of a small number of spiritually-alive men and women in whose hearts burned the light of true faith. Little noticed, as we may suppose, by the official religious leaders of the day and little involved in the momentous secular upheavals at that time in the state of Israel, they were among the Lord's true disciples in a spiritually-corrupt period of the church. Their ministry was one of waiting on God in secret and, by fastings and prayers, of pleading with God to bring that dreary age to an end and to usher into this needy world One who would be its Light and its Glory.

The facts given here would be interesting enough in themselves if we knew no more of this lively band of praying saints. The curtain which is drawn back for a moment to reveal these spiritual worthies might easily have been again re-drawn to conceal the outcome of their prayers. But God's Spirit has graciously given us much more. He shows us also their reward and the marvellous way in which their faith and prayers are heard in heaven. Never did praying saints more fully receive their hearts' desire than did these precious Jewish believers in Jerusalem.

Led by divine guidance, as they were, both Simeon and Anna came into the temple at the very hour when Joseph and Mary brought in the infant Jesus to 'present him to the Lord' (*Luke* 2:22, 27, 38). According to their faith it was done unto them. Both Simeon and Anna were richly rewarded at the end of their long life of prayer by a sight of the Child whom they well knew to be the 'light to lighten the Gentiles and the glory of God's people Israel' (*Luke* 2:32). The long night of Old Testament times was now at an end. The church of God was about to 'lengthen her cords and strengthen her stakes' (*Isa.* 54:2). In this Child all nations were now to be blessed.

It is little wonder, as Simeon takes up the tiny form of Jesus in his arms, that he blesses God for the privilege given to him of seeing and holding to himself the Lord from heaven whose blood would 'sprinkle many nations' (*Isa.* 52:15). As Simeon prepares to depart from the stage of life, his life's work now done and well done, he blesses God. Then, having announced prophetically to Mary that the sword of grief would one day pierce her heart (surely a reference to seeing her Son on the Cross), he summarizes Christ's ministry as one which would turn the lives of multitudes upside down. So exits this man of God.

Anna too thanks the Lord and goes back to the band of prayer-warriors to announce the arrival of the great Messiah himself and, therefore too, the end of an age. These are they who wrestled with God, and prevailed. They are an inspiration to all God's people to live well in a cloudy and dark day and, in the worst of times, to hope against hope in the sure promises of God. It would be good to learn in our own day that the same faith and prayerfulness were alive and active. Happy would we be be if there were at least some mighty wrestlers with God. Oh, to hear of a group somewhere, no larger perhaps than a cloud the size of a man's hand, of Christians engaged in this secret ministry of earnest intercession! No service for God would surely be more precious than that of men and women devoted to a life of prayer, and importuning heaven for a fresh visitation of grace upon all our churches!

There is a host of good reasons why Christians with leisure to do so should set themselves, as Simeon and Anna did, to pray in these days with all prayer and supplication, with strong crying and tears, and with all the energies of their soul for God to revive us all again. It is one of the chief challenges of this hour.

We do not suggest that the case of Christians praying in secret today would be precisely parallel to that of Simeon and Anna secretly praying for God to bless his church in their time. *They* had a special revelation of the soon coming of Christ in the flesh; *we* have no such revelation of a visitation of God in our land. *They* prayed for the coming of the Son of God and for his incarnation; *we* for his Spirit to 'lift up a standard against the enemy who has come in like a flood' (*Isa.* 59:19). The two situations are in some respects different.

But in essence their position and ours are surely the same. *They* lived in a dreary age when little of God's power was visible in the church; *we* too live in a time when the arm of God is not being made bare in preaching. *They* lived in a day when true religion was at a low ebb; so also do *we*.

Just about every ingenious artifice that the wit of man can devise has been tried in a frenzied effort to inject more life into churches in our Western world. We do not offer this criticism to discourage effort for God's cause but to call attention to the sad reality that, for all these multiplied forms of evangelism, little has happened of which it could be said, 'This is the finger of God'. The sobering fact which must surely be faced is that little of the *power* of *God* has attended the machinery of our human endeavour. The *one* thing which really matters has been conspicuous by its absence: power to change the condition of the world all around us. Society sleeps on in its deep sleep of death.

Though we do not have revelations or prophecies today as Simeon and Anna did, we do have encouragement to hope for great things from God in our times. In the second half of the twentieth century, the gracious hand of God was sowing truth in the earth everywhere. There are today more good books of sound theology in the world than probably ever before in the history of mankind.

Here surely is the spur we need to prompt our souls to look to God for a fresh shower of blessing on his church commensurate with the extent of this recovery of sound doctrine. The doctrine is essential; but if it is to shake society out of its slumbers this theology must become incandescent in men's souls as they preach it and as they hear it preached. The fire of truth is burning, but the bellows are needed to blow up the flame till it becomes a conflagration.

It is precisely at this point that we need today the ministry of an Anna and of a Simeon. The call goes out to all who are zealous for God's cause and who have leisure. Let them see the vision of a ministry of fervent prayer to God *in secret*. Let every saint who has health and strength to do so set aside quality time for exercising themselves in this secret work within the closet. Let them cry out mightily to God, 'O Lord, save thy people and remember thy holy promises! Why should the heathen say, "Where is their God"?'

The ministry in secret of Simeon and Anna was one of the most significant events on earth in its time. It was not chronicled by the historians who wrote of Julius Caesar's conquests in Britain a little earlier. But it was chronicled in those books of God on high, whose records will be reckoned precious when all the volumes of mere men are at last cast into the fire.

Simeon and Anna were content to exercise a ministry which few but God knew of. But they kept firmly at their devotions till their heart's desire was at last given to them. Their ministry in secret was at length rewarded openly. Will anyone, following their example, take up the ministry of Simeon and Anna today?

THE LIFE OF GRACE
– LIVING FOR GOD

4

Godliness

A sure mark of true religion must always be godliness. It is not morality first of all. Morality must be rooted and grounded in evangelical holiness, or else it will quickly become self-righteousness and pharisaism. True religion does not consist mainly in the possession of gifts, either natural or spiritual. We must always preserve the clear distinction between gifts and grace. It is here that we are all in danger of going astray badly. To speak in tongues, to perform wonders, to have healing powers is not the essence of true Christianity. A man may, like Judas, possess such spiritual gifts and yet be without grace.

What is true of spiritual gifts may be also said of natural gifts. Powers of speaking and of intellect are not the essence of religion. We must never suggest that cleverness or learning or education are the main things. They are very good when found in a man of God. But they are exceedingly harmful when not sanctified. Thomas Halyburton learned that lesson as a young man when an old minister told him, 'Unsanctified learning has done much harm to the church.' Neither morality, nor giftedness, nor eloquence, nor cleverness is the marrow of Christianity; but godliness is.

Godliness is not easy to define in a word or two. It is a hunger in the heart of a renewed man for God. It is a strange consuming passion in the soul of a believer for nearness to God. It was said of one of the philosophers that he was a 'God-intoxicated man'. The phrase is worth using at least to show what godliness is in the soul of a true Christian. We are not interested in whether it was aptly used of the philosopher or not. But here is the essence of true holiness of life as it is always found, more or less, in all converted persons. With this yearning for God in the heart there is nothing to compare in importance in all the universe. The measure of a man is the measure of this appetite for union and communion with the living God. Small appetite proves small grace; large appetite proves much grace; no appetite shows there is no grace at all.

There is something violent about a soul in love with God. The Bible witnesses to this fact. Abraham is ready to offer up his son as a bloody sacrifice for no other reason than that he hears this to be the will of God. The naked will of God is all he lives by. Lesser Christians could scarcely bear such a test of Divine sovereignty. Most of us would ask God for reasons. But eminent, shining piety, like Abraham's, is ready to hazard all for the love it bears to the august and dread Being of God. It obeys even when it does not understand. It is God's glory to conceal his reasons from us. It is the mark of true godliness never to ask for them.

This is the essence of true love to God: 'I delight to do thy will, O my God.' Not always to understand it, but always to do it. That is the difference between godliness and fanaticism. Fanaticism strives to impress by its very extremeness. Godliness is anxious solely to do God's will, whether others see it or not. Godliness does the will of God so that the right hand does not see what the left is doing. Fanaticism always blows a trumpet in one way or another, and it is not regulated by the will of God.

Fanatics are fascinating people. In a way they shame us for our mediocrity and show us something new and awesome in religion. Madame Guyon stitched the Name of Jesus to her bare flesh. John of the Cross had nails in his shirt in order (as he imagined) to mortify the flesh. Saint Teresa swooned when she had her rapturous visions, as she thought, of Christ. Simon Stylites stood all his life on the top of a high pillar – for God's glory as he supposed. St Antony lived as a solitary hermit in the Egyptian desert that he might contemplate the mysteries of the faith. For a moment we are awe-struck when we think of these professed Christians. But when sanity returns we recall that more has to be said.

The fanatics go terribly wrong in one point. They go beyond the will of God. They live beyond and outside the revealed will of God. They have forgotten that 'to obey is better than sacrifice', and that 'whatsoever is not of faith is sin'. But there is in true godliness (and this is not to deny that some at least of the fanatics were truly converted persons, though misled) what we might call a kind of 'inward fanaticism', so to speak. By this we mean that godliness in its higher, stronger, maturer expressions and exercises is awe-inspiring and disconcerting to us in a similar sort of way to the fanatics. The biblical saints illustrate the point. Noah built the ark for no less than one hundred and twenty years. Moses' zeal for God's glory leads him to pray: 'Blot me, I pray thee, out of thy book which thou hast written' (*Exod.* 32:32). Elijah is content to be fed by ravens. John the Baptist lives on locusts and wild honey.

Paul would fain be 'accursed from Christ' if he may but save his Jewish brethren (*Rom.* 9:3). Of all these holy men it could be said, their meat and drink was to do the will of God, to please him, to finish their work, to approve themselves to God in all things. It is godliness that inspires them. It is what lifts them above the common order of men, even Christian men.

It is not only the biblical saints that are like that. The same character is to be found in the best Christians of all ages. The best saints have always had a profound, all-absorbing preoccupation with the knowledge of God. Take Augustine: 'I desire to know God and my soul. Nothing more? No, nothing at all.' These are the words of a religious genius. He was a dungeon of learning, a master of rhetoric, a perfect Latinist, an expert in Roman Law. But his gifts of mind are not settled on secular themes. He passes beyond them all to the Being of God. Only in knowing God is his soul brought into the haven of rest. 'Our heart is restless till we find our rest in Thee.'

All is dross that is not found in God, that leads not to God, that lifts us not up to God. This is what condemns the purely academic person, the pure scholar. He is an idolater at heart. He rises no higher than his studies. His darkened heart is in love with the creature, and is content to terminate on his researches, on the secular level. It is a squalid and unworthy terminus for the mind of any man. It is to miss the wood for the trees. The unstudied Christian is higher in the scale by far than the studied unbeliever. The ignorant Christian rises to the Source of all, which is God. The scholar without Christ is a 'fool' (*Psa.* 14:1) because all his learning does not bring him to penetrate the secret of the universe, which is to be found in Christ alone.

Calvin begins his *Institutes* with the point which Augustine made much earlier: 'Our wisdom, in so far as it ought to be deemed true and solid wisdom, consists almost entirely of two parts: the knowledge of God and of ourselves.' These are the first words of that great book. It is not that Calvin is simply picking up the threads where Augustine had left them a thousand years before. That he does do. But it is not the artificial effect of a self-conscious imitator. There was inevitability in it. Calvin's concept of theology is the very practical one that it is only truth from God that promotes godliness in man. This comes out very clearly from the whole title to the *Institutes*, which begins: 'The Basic Teaching of the Christian Religion, comprising almost the sum of godliness and whatever it is necessary to know on the doctrine of salvation.' That is the burden of the matter for Calvin: truth in order to godliness. It is the echo of Paul's phrase, 'the doctrine which is according to godliness' (*1 Tim.* 6:3). This emphasis is the hall-mark of all the greatest theological writing and all the best evangelical preaching.

Herman Bavinck was stating what had been believed by all his best predecessors when he wrote in his *Inaugural Address* as Professor of Systematic Theology in the Free University of Amsterdam: 'Religion, the fear of God, must therefore be the element which inspires and animates all theological investigations. That must be the pulse beat of the science.' It is the same, basically, as what we have in the more homely words of M'Cheyne, that God does not require of us great learning but great likeness to Jesus Christ. At first sight it might appear that Bavinck is at variance with M'Cheyne. The former is talking about the importance of theological study: the latter about Christian living. But both are entirely agreed in this, that godliness – the fear of God, likeness to Christ – must be regarded as at the root of all that is best in the experience of the believer. At this one thing we aim above all else.

It should be the thoughtful and conscious aim of the Christian to grow in godliness. The immature Christian is content with little morsels of the knowledge of God. The young Christian is delighted with his books and his grasp of the orthodox creed. This is right and proper in its own way. But we must go on to perfection and to spiritual manhood in the personal, experimental enjoyment of the knowledge of God. Our books, our sermons, our communion seasons, our fellowship meetings of all kinds must be valued by us only as they lead us to a deeper knowledge of God himself. The aim is not personal pleasure but personal godliness.

It is difficult to measure growth in the knowledge of God because it is many-sided and comes to light in a variety of ways. But we suggest that there are in Scripture a number of marks of the maturing soul. For one thing, weariness with sin and with ourselves. The soul that is in love with God must be increasingly out of love with its sinful self. The product of this is meekness. No wonder Moses was the meekest man on earth. Job, too, was the greatest saint then alive (according to the judgment of God). Both men were remarkable for their meekness. They were so near the throne that they abhorred themselves in sackcloth and ashes.

Another test of growth in godliness is a developed moral sensitivity. The holier the Christian, the more he feels the spirituality and strictness of the Moral Law of God. That is why Calvin spends such a large part of his *Institutes* in expounding the Decalogue. Indeed, the *Westminster Shorter Catechism* takes up more time on the Ten Commandments than it does on basic theology. Developed Christian godliness is godliness in detail, obedience to the jot and tittle of the Law as well as to the broad general principles of Christian morality. It will not do to criticize this Catechism as though it were badly balanced. The balance is deliberately and consciously made. The Catechism is not just to inform the head but to reform the heart and to mould the life.

We mention a third evidence of growing piety. It is fear of God. Careless Christians have low views of the strictness of God. They treat him as one of themselves. He is welcomed as a Father, but scarcely as a Judge before whom we shall all one day stand when 'every mouth shall be stopped'. Growth in godliness will always correct low views of God. Aaron had low views of God when he made the golden calf. But Moses' soul burned with holy indignation to the extent that he broke the tables of stone. He could not rest till the guilty had been slain and the calf ground to powder. He was higher in godliness than Aaron by many diameters. That was the great difference between them. Both were saved men, both were heirs of glory: but Moses was far more in the fear of the Lord. He excelled in godliness all who lived in his day.

All the saved are godly. Conversion plants the seed of God in the heart. But the godly have much need of further godliness. Perhaps one of the deepest needs we all have as Christians today is this: to catch the vision which Calvinists in their best days have always cherished of the serious call to a devout and holy life.

We tend to say 'saved' and 'unsaved'. But the saved are themselves called to 'perfect holiness in the fear of God'. As one of the old divines put it: 'The lowest degree of grace will bring salvation to you, but not much glory to God.' We would be the better if we lived in the light of M'Cheyne's expression: 'Live so as to be missed when you die.'

5

Union and Communion with Christ

Not the least reason why we should love Jesus Christ is that he has united us to himself forever if we are true believers. It is an unspeakable blessing to have our guilt removed by the blood of the Redeemer. But to have him eternally as our Head and Husband, united to us both in grace and glory, is a favour no less wonderful and mysterious.

This union with Christ is represented in Scripture by a variety of illustrations. In some passages it is compared to the relationship of the head to the body. The church is a living organism in which all the members have a particular part to play in promoting the health and prosperity of the whole.

But, more importantly still, all the members are united to Christ as their controlling intelligence. Christ's headship over the church is to be total and complete. The constant care of the church must be to be subject to Christ in all things (*Eph.* 5:24). The church does not make up her own articles of belief, nor does she lay down her own principles of worship or government. In everything she is bound by the Word of Christ. It is inherent in the relationship which believers have to Christ that they must have no other doctrines, practices or agendas but such as he has laid down for them as their Head.

A second illustration of Scripture to depict this union of believers with Christ is that of a temple (*Eph.* 2:21, *1 Pet.* 2:5). Christ is the chief corner-stone, and believers are living and spiritual stones fitted into the building. The Spirit of God indwells the vast edifice and fills it with his presence. In the course of history this building is 'growing' (*Eph.* 2:21) and will not be complete till all the elect are gathered in and Christ returns.

This portrait of the church's union with her Lord draws attention to the holiness and spirituality of the people of God. The great characteristics of the church in this world are her moral excellence and likeness to Christ. *God* will ensure that she 'grows'; she must ensure that she maintains and safeguards her own holiness and spiritual dignity. For as the Lord Jesus Christ is, so is she in this world (*1 John* 4:17). A temple is not just a building, but a sacred place consecrated to the worship of God. No influence must induce the people of God to forget what they are.

A third picture found in the Bible to explain the union of Christ with believers is that of the vine and its branches (*John* 15:1ff). Our souls are as completely dependent on the supply of grace from Christ as is the vine on the rising of its sap to bring life and growth. The church's mission is to 'bring forth fruit' to the glory of God. Christians are to be visible saints, and their life is to be devoted to one ambition, glorifying God and spreading the knowledge of his truth among men.

If we are to become more fruitful we must expect God to 'prune' our lives with the sharp knife of sanctifying experiences. Sin must be dealt with, our hearts become more pure in their affection for God, our fruitfulness be increased by the constant daily attention to these ministrations of the heavenly Gardener.

All this is implied in the familiar illustration given by our Lord himself, who repeatedly urges us to 'abide in him' and to 'abide in his love', the condition of which is that we must keep his commandments (*John* 15:10).

The above portrait of our union with Christ makes it clear that the Christian life is one of experience of God's gracious dealings. The gardener's knife is intrusive. It cuts away part of what we love and cling to. But all such humbling and chastening experiences are beneficial. God takes nothing away from the Christian without giving something better. We lose in order to gain. There cannot be much fruitfulness without much experience of God's sanctifying, and sometimes sharp, dealings.

The false Christian may appear as good as others for a time, but he has no real union with Christ, and sooner or later he will drop off and fall away. This, sadly, is not confined to the single case of Judas Iscariot. The Saviour's words come as a wholesome warning to us all: 'Every branch in me that beareth not fruit he taketh away . . . If a man abide not in me, he is cast forth as a branch, and is withered; and men gather them, and cast them into the fire, and they are burned' (*John* 15:2, 6). We shall see these dead branches removed if we keep our eyes open.

The most amazing picture of all used by God to depict the believer's union with Jesus Christ is that of marriage. It is a figure which occurs again and again in the Word of

God, notably in the Song of Solomon, in Psalm 45, in Hosea, in Ephesians 5 and in Revelation 21, where the church is referred to as 'the Lamb's wife' (*Rev.* 21:9).

No greater honour could be given to us as believers than to be referred to as the 'wife' of the glorious Son of God. It is a term implying a thousand comforting and reassuring thoughts to those who love Jesus. He and we are 'one'. This is true of our body and of our soul. 'Your bodies are the members of Christ' (*1 Cor.* 615). 'He that is joined unto the Lord is one spirit' (*1 Cor.* 6:17).

Christ will never divorce his spouse nor cast her out of house and home. He will never repent of his choice of us to be his Bride. He has taken us 'for better, for worse'. Best of all, we need not say of this marriage that it is good only 'till death us do part'. 'Thy Maker is thy husband' (*Isa.* 54:5). Christ will be our Head and Husband long after the mountains and hills about us shall have been removed forever (*Isa.* 54:10).

The relationship of union between the church and Christ is 'a great mystery' (*Eph.* 5:32). It is certain that we shall never grasp perfectly in this life what is meant by the statement: 'We are members of his body, of his flesh and of his bones' (*Eph.* 5:30). The Last Adam had his Eve in his mind's eye before the first Adam was created. In the course of time, Christ, who 'loved the church', 'gave himself for it' (*Eph.* 5:25). His intention was, in time, to sanctify her 'by the word', that in eternity 'he might present it to himself a glorious church, not having spot or wrinkle or any such thing' (*Eph.* 5:26, 27).

There is a day coming when the church will be worthy of her Christ and when she shall appear to all the universe 'as a bride adorned for her husband' (*Rev.* 21:2). The church has often gone through pain and suffering here below, but on her wedding day all her sorrow will be forgotten. One moment in the presence of the Bridegroom will more than recompense her for many thousand years of persecution and misrepresentation.

The union which we have with Christ is the closest of all unions and is in some mysterious ways similar to that sublime union between the persons of the great Godhead. So Christ says to his Father: 'And the glory which thou gavest me I have given them; that they may be one, even as we are one; I in them, and thou in me, that they may be made perfect in one; and that the world may know that thou hast sent me, and hast loved them, as thou hast loved me' (*John* 17:22–23).

The Lord Jesus will be to us not just a Saviour, but also a Husband. As a Saviour he has delivered us from all our sins and miseries. As a Husband he has lifted us up to the highest privilege conceivable to any creature: to be united in conjugal love eternally to One who is God.

The prayer of Christ above quoted will surely not be fulfilled until the church is all made up and every elect member gathered in. Then the God-hating, Christ-rejecting world will see with its own astonished eyes that Christ is indeed the true Messiah and that the church is indeed his chosen Bride. The prayer of our great Husband is daily coming closer to its fulfilment. 'The voice of the archangel' and 'the trump of God' (*1 Thess.* 4:16) will summon the righteous from their graves to put on their wedding garments. Christ and his people will then have their union publicly consummated in the presence of God and all angels. No disappointment could ever match that of the foolish virgins who will miss the joys of that heavenly marriage because they have no oil of grace and so find the 'door shut' (*Matt.* 25:10). The warning is good for us all.

As Christians we are on a journey in this life that leads to our wedding day, and we would do well to remind ourselves of it frequently. This view of life will compensate us for the losses and crosses which are part of our present earthly experience. But we shall not much care about the occasional rainy day if we keep in view the warmth of Christ's embrace when the day of his espousals is come. If we suffer for and with him now we shall sit with him on his throne at last. It is easy to bear with the reproaches of men if we remember that all our detractors and persecutors will give an account to our Lord in the end. Christ is not the husband to let his Bride lie under unkind aspersions for ever. Those who speak evil of Christ's church will answer for it, whoever they are. 'He shall strike through kings in the day of his wrath' (*Psa.* 110:5).

We make a distinction between our union with Christ and our communion with him. The union is always there and cannot be broken. But the communion which we have with Christ in this life is our felt, conscious enjoyment of his love. This is by no means constant, but varies from day to day and from hour to hour. The mature believer's supreme desire is, as was George Whitefield's, to have the enjoyment of a 'felt Christ'.

6

No Mere Memory

Half of all our pleasures and our pains come to us through the memory. The memory is a mental camera which receives and stores the experiences of life and then later provides us with an album of recollections, the opening of which can move us to tears of either sorrow or joy. The memory enables us to relive our past life in the present, to compare the present with the past and to compile a private manual of collected wisdom for the future.

The longer we live the larger the manual of experience becomes. A fool learns nothing from his past life; but a wise man has learnt the art of continually checking and cross-checking his own behaviour. His aim is to avoid repeating his painful past mistakes. Memory is his constant reference book. His ambition is to become perfect in all his ways. In this labour his memory is a most faithful secretary and accountant, now knocking on the door of conscience and now turning up the ledger of former failures. Without the aid of memory how could we ever make progress in holiness?

So helpful a thing is memory that we must count it as one of life's truly great blessings from God our Maker. It is given to us, not merely for the benefit of our life as students at school or in college, but, much more, to equip us to be good scholars in Christ's kingdom. It is a choice part of the image of God in our soul and, if used aright, will enrich and ennoble our whole life, more or less to the end. Conscience is the policeman of the soul; but memory is the soul's librarian.

The sweetest part of memory is the recollection of God's gracious dealings with us in the past. The believer's life is etched with memories of the good things which God has done for him over the years: here a merciful provision, there a timely intervention, everywhere a constant supply of grace, mercy and peace. Huge landmarks stand above the horizon of a believer's life as he looks back: the experience of conversion, the entrance of the soul into full assurance (often after a struggle), victory over a score of fiery temptations, comfort in loss, material provision in poverty, escape from snares, and amazing answers to prayer in times of need.

Memory has written these experiences down forever on the table of the heart. We have but to touch the keys of thought and a cluster of emotions crowds into the mind of a Christian. No wonder God has said, 'Thou shalt remember all the way which the LORD thy God led thee' (*Deut.* 8:2)!

In this life it is to be expected that many a painful and humbling event will force itself back upon our memory. There have been times in which we sinned grievously against God. On such occasions we forget ourselves and put a life-long memory-blot on our livery. Or else we failed to mortify both tongue and temper. Such memories must abase us in the dust before the God whom we love and serve. But even our sad lapses must not be allowed to crush us. The guilt of our worst sins is covered with the atoning blood. We weep over our past failures, but not as those who have no gracious Saviour to comfort us.

Before we ever sink into self-pity at the remembrance of our past sorrows and miseries, we might do well to remember how much sadder and darker must have been the memory of others before us. Adam, who in his first estate had a more perfect memory than all of us, lived almost a thousand years with the bitter recollection of the one sin which ruined the world and brought death upon all his posterity. How often must our forefather have gone over in his mind those few guilty moments of his life when he ate from the tree and disobeyed God. How many thousand times must he have wept to recall his guilty act and bemoan the shame that made him stitch together his worthless suit of fig-leaves! How often must Eve, our first mother, have wept hot tears of regret when she remembered over a long life-time how, as Adam's help-meet, she so unhelpfully acted the part of his seducer to sin!

Their comfort in repentance was the One who should come to crush Satan underfoot in the course of time. The same Christ is our comfort today as we also blush with shame at our many falls and foolish failings in the past.

Did Christ himself have painful memories? The question forces itself upon us. Unquestionably our blessed Saviour, perfect in memory as in all else, had a full book of sad recollections in this life. His sensitivity was that of a perfect man, wholly alive to the requirement of God's law to love our neighbour as ourself. How full a cup must he have had of bitter memories of the cruel hatred of those who ought to have recognized, loved and worshipped him! If we desire a model of how to go on to the end of our life's vocation in spite of man's unkindness, we need look nowhere else than at this Man of Sorrows who was everywhere contradicted and misrepresented.

Not the least of this world's ungenerous acts in its treatment of Jesus Christ was the way in which men sent him to his death with a memory veritably plastered with ten thousand insults and cruelties which he had suffered at their hands. No doubt, as our Lord hung on the cross he could refer to those sorrows in the words of the prophet: 'Remembering mine affliction and my misery, the wormwood and the gall. My soul hath them still in remembrance, and is humbled in me' (*Lam.* 3:19–20). Our Lord, however, looked over the head of all his miseries to 'the joy that was set before him' (*Heb.* 12:2), a joy now completed in the Father's presence, free from all pain of past suffering. To this same joy his people will come who overcome as he overcame. There are no painful memories in heaven. Whatever memories we shall have in that blessed place they will all be sugared over and honeyed through and through with the love of Christ.

The bad news for Christless sinners is that God has an infallible memory and cannot forget their sins. Before his all-knowing eye the evil deeds of godless men are 'written with a pen of iron and with the point of a diamond' (*Jer.* 17:1). The sins of evil men cannot be covered by anything but the blood of Christ. They are not concealed or cloaked by priestly absolution or by masses, by holy water or by many prayers, by knowledge of Reformation creeds or by the reading of many Puritan books. If men hope to conceal their guiltiness from God's eye by anything other than the merits of a crucified Christ alone, they are feeding on the ashes of self-deception. A sinner's forgotten sins will rise up to meet him in the day of death like a swarm of locusts. They will feed on his flesh like fire.

Memory will play a large and important part in the eternal punishment of those who die out of Christ. So much is clear from the words spoken to the Rich Man in hell: 'Son, remember that thou in thy lifetime receivedst thy good things and likewise Lazarus evil things; but now he is comforted and thou art tormented' (*Luke* 16:25). Could any message be more doleful for one whose good things were now all in the past and who had no more experience of those good things beyond the bare recollection of them and the heat of an eternal fire to tell him that these good things were now gone forever?

So memory, like the 'worm that dieth not', will gnaw at the soul of the damned to all eternity. Once let the unsaved, unwashed soul pass over the threshold of death and it must be faced forever with a host of memories of good things now eventually lost! Oh that the sinner would stop now, in this life, to remember that his present blessings will mock him in hell-fire if he loves them more than God! Ten million blessings of time and sense are worth throwing away to get Christ and to arrive at last in glory with him.

Our God, most thankfully, remembers other things too besides men's sins. The very first reference to memory in the Bible is not of man's remembering but of God's: 'And God remembered Noah, and every living thing, and all the cattle that was with him in the ark' (*Gen.* 8:1). Even 'cattle' are remembered by God. Once the wicked were swept away by the great Flood, so we are here instructed, God called to his own mind his promise to believing Noah. A new world must now appear, as if from the ashes of the old. Noah and his family must be fed, clothed and cared for, because so God had faithfully promised.

God cannot lie, die or deny himself. And he cannot forget his own promises to those who believe in him: 'I will remember my covenant which is between me and you' (*Gen.* 9:15). The various promises of God are like so many mansions in a great house for believers to live and rest in all the days of their life here in this world. So Peter speaks of God's 'exceeding great and precious promises: that by these ye might be partakers of the divine nature, having escaped the corruption that is in the world through lust' (*2 Pet.* 1:4).

God's promises to us must be the furniture of our minds and memories so long as we are in this life. To live by faith is to live by the promises of God. Just as the promise held good for Noah when the rain fell and the floods arose, while the old world became submerged and all visible objects became engulfed in the waters of the Flood, so God's promise of eternal life and salvation will survive the collapse of all earthly things. The promises of God will outlive the universe. They will hold good when at last 'the elements shall melt with fervent heat', and the world as we now know it is 'burned up' (*2 Pet.* 3:10). God will remember his promises to those who have been in covenant with him here below: 'For this is as the waters of Noah unto me: for as I have sworn that the waters of Noah should no more go over the earth; so have I sworn that I would not be wroth with thee, nor rebuke thee. For the mountains shall depart, and the hills be removed;

but my kindness shall not depart from thee, neither shall the covenant of my peace be removed, saith the Lord that hath mercy on thee' (*Isa.* 54:9–10).

The one thing which God will not remember is that which he wills to forget: the sin of those who believe in Jesus Christ his Son: 'I will remember their sin no more' (*Jer.* 31:34; *Heb.* 10:17).

But will believers not remember their sins forever in glory? No doubt they will, since their new song has reference to Christ's cross and they sing to him in redemptive language: 'Thou wast slain, and hast redeemed us to God by thy blood out of every kindred, and tongue, and people and nation' (*Rev.* 5:9). But their remembrance of past sin in glory will bring no grief to them because it no longer offends a propitiated God, who sees the blood and passes over their guilt. The remembrance of sins by the redeemed in glory will but lift still higher their notes of praise to their Redeemer.

7

Living with Our Limitations

The Christian life is in many ways a paradoxical life. By this we mean that the Christian's life is full of apparent contradictions. As believers we are 'in the world but not of it' (*John* 17:14–15). Sin is in us but we are not in sin. We belong to a world of perfection shortly to be revealed, but we are at present full of imperfections. We rejoice and yet we also groan. Heaven is begun in our hearts, but hell has not yet entirely lost its influence upon us. We are surrounded by angels and yet also tempted by devils. We are perfectly justified but not perfectly sanctified.

The Christian's life in this world is a sort of interim-life or in-between-life. We are not what we were but we are also not what we would be and shall be. We are absent from the Christ whom we long to see because we are at present still coming up out of the wilderness. Heaven is in our hearts and in our mind's eye but we are as yet still far from home and amid many dangerous enemies. We are therefore at peace with God but must always be on the watch. We are safe, but only so long as we keep awake. We cannot lose our salvation but we may, through carelessness or idleness, lose some of our reward (*2 John* 8; *Rev.* 3:11).

We are at present in a state of transition. God has not finished his work in us as yet. But when God's work concerning us is complete we shall be all that we ought to be and all that we now long to be. 'He knoweth the way that I take: when he hath tried me, I shall come forth as gold' (*Job* 23:10). As yet, we are still like ore that is being smelted, or earthen pots being glazed in the furnace, or fruit on the tree which is not fully ripe.

The Christian life in this present world is one in which we are being 'processed' or prepared. A daily alteration is going on within us which is not going on in the non-Christian. He is changing only in the sense that the principles of sin and death, which were in him at birth, are gaining ground on him and will one day overtake him. But there are forces and powers at work in the believer which are raising him to ever-new heights of spiritual life and knowledge. 'We all, with open face beholding as in a glass the glory of the Lord, are changed into the same image from glory to glory, even as by the Spirit of the Lord' (*2 Cor.* 3:18).

It is remarkable that the Scriptures repeatedly say that the Christian is now in a state which is advancing and progressing. We go, so the Bible says, 'from glory to glory' (*2 Cor.* 3:18). We advance 'from strength to strength' (*Psa.* 84:7). We receive out of Christ's fulness 'grace for grace' (*John* 1:16). Our life is progressive in terms also of the degree of our believing. It is moving 'from faith to faith' (*Rom.* 1:17). All such expressions are a reminder to us that our present life is one of process, maturing, preparation and development. The fully mature state has not yet arrived, but it is in view even now while we are still green and unripe. All our experiences of growing are pledges of perfection in a better state and in a better world.

The Christian's life is therefore the reverse of the non-Christian's. The one is moving towards perfection in glory; the other to final and irretrievable loss. The believer will in the end be ripe for heaven; the other for eternal misery in hell. The one is soon to be a 'vessel of mercy unto honour'; the other a 'vessel of wrath fitted to destruction' (*Rom.* 9:21–23). Soon, all the good things which godless men enjoy will be but haunting memories of good things lost forever. In their ears will sound the doleful words, 'Son, remember that thou in thy lifetime receivedst thy good things' (*Luke* 16:25).

The believer's present life is therefore like the spring-time. He can look forward to summer days coming soon. The sinner's life is like the autumn of the year. The plentiful fruits which he now enjoys will not last. Winter days are at hand.

The more the Christian lives close to Christ, the more he will become aware of the paradoxical nature of his life here below. No-one expresses it so vividly as the Apostle Paul in his Second Epistle to the Corinthians: 'We are troubled on every side, yet not distressed; we are perplexed, but not in despair; Persecuted, but not forsaken; cast down, but not destroyed; Always bearing about in the body the dying of the Lord Jesus, that the life also of Jesus might be made manifest in our body. For we which live are always delivered unto death for Jesus' sake, that the life also of Jesus might be made manifest in our mortal flesh. So then death worketh in us, but life in you' (*2 Cor.* 4:8–12).

The minister of the gospel, especially, must expect to feel this strange fact in experience. We are 'always bearing about in the body the dying of the Lord Jesus, that the life also of Jesus might be made manifest in our body' (*2 Cor.* 4:10). The Christian minister, more than others, feels the paradox of life in this world. The strange experiences of those who are called to serve Jesus Christ in such a fallen world as this are reflected in terms like these: '[We live] by honour and dishonour, by evil report and good report: as deceivers and yet true, as unknown and yet well known; as dying, and, behold, we live; as chastened, and not killed; As sorrowful, yet always rejoicing; as poor, yet making many rich; as having nothing, and yet possessing all things' (*2 Cor.* 6:8–10). Who but a spiritual person could begin to make sense of such a statement?

These experiences are all a part of the paradox of a believer's life in this world. By some he is as much loved as by others he is hated. At some times he is as much filled with joy as at others he is with sadness. 'As the sufferings of Christ abound in us, so our consolation also aboundeth by Christ' (*2 Cor.* 1:5). 'We were pressed out of measure, above strength, insomuch that we despaired even of life: but we had the sentence of death in ourselves, that we should not trust in ourselves, but in God, which raiseth the dead: who delivered us from so great a death, and does deliver: in whom we trust that he will yet deliver us' (*2 Cor.* 1:8–10). The believer is a mystery to himself much of the time.

The paradox of the believer's life does not end with his outward experiences but it is a daily part of his knowledge of his own sinful heart and of his sinful past. The Christian knows full well that God has forgiven all the sins of his pre-Christian life. But there is a sense in which we must still sorrow to think of our old sins and try to put right the harm which they did to others. There is a sense in which it is a sin to forget our old sins. What else can Peter mean by warning against the example of some who had 'forgotten that they were purged from their old sins' (*2 Pet.* 1:9)? It is clear that Paul had not forgotten his old sins. Even at the end of his wonderful ministry he still remembered that he 'was *before* a blasphemer, and a persecutor, and injurious' (*1 Tim.* 1:13). Such thoughts, when they are in biblical balance, do not crush us with fear or despair but they refresh our sense of gratitude to God for his free grace.

So too with our present sins. They are a burden to us, and yet, when viewed in the light of Christ's cross, they do not drive us to despair. Indwelling sin humbles the believer but, if seen in the context of the blood of Jesus, it cannot overwhelm him. We take sides against our sins and we approve God's disapproval of them. We approve God's law and applaud it as 'holy, just and good' (*Rom.* 7:12) and so we judge our own sins and frown on our own acts of disobedience. We wish, as Christians, that we had never sinned and we wish that we might never sin again; but in the same breath we admit that we are very sinful still.

The difference between the true believer and the hypocrite is seen in the way he views his own sins and the sins of others. To the hypocrite the sins of others are great and his own small. He is confident that the fig-leaves of his own religious performances fully cover over his own minor blemishes. The thought of his heart is, 'God, I thank thee that I am not as other men are, extortioners . . . adulterers' (*Luke* 18:11).

Far different is the real believer who knows his own heart. He considers his own sins great and those of others small by comparison. The better the Christian the humbler his view of himself and the more generous his praise of his brethren. How paradoxical is the language of Paul: 'I am less than the least of all saints' (*Eph.* 3:8) and 'the chief of sinners' (*1 Tim.* 1:15). Who but a Christian could follow this way of putting himself so low? None of the sons of men of whom we read in the Bible are so great as Paul (we of course exclude Christ, who is the Son of God); yet none speaks so meanly of himself or so disapprovingly of his own sins.

Part of the mystery of Paul's modesty is in the high view he has of God's law and in the serious attitude he has to indwelling sin. We wish all believers had so high a view of the claims of obedience to law upon their lives. Low views of law lead to low views of sin in a believer's life. The next consequence is that we easily live with our sinful selves and do not groan to be delivered from our residual depravity, which is nothing short of residual hatred of God in our souls.

The Christian is not meant to be at ease with his imperfections in this life, but to labour patiently at perfection.

8

'No Cross, No Crown'

There is no getting to heaven without suffering. Those (and they are many) who hope to come to heaven without pain in this life are hoping for what Christ never promised. Such a hope is based on fancy not on faith, for faith rests on divine revelation. But there are no promises that any shall have heaven without affliction. The only exceptions are elect infants dying in infancy. Of these, and of those not yet born, it might be said: 'Yea, better is he than both they, which hath not yet been, who hath not seen the evil work that is done under the sun' (*Eccles.* 4:3). Those for whom Christ shed his blood, who die in the womb, pass at once into glory. All others for whom Christ died go to glory by a rougher road.

It is no kindness to pretend to those newly converted or to those whom we evangelize that the way to heaven is easy. Christ himself did not conceal from his hearers the thorns that lie before all his disciples: 'I send you forth as sheep in the midst of wolves . . . Beware of men for they will deliver you up . . . The brother shall deliver up the brother to death . . . Ye shall be hated of all men for my name's sake . . . It is enough for the disciple that he be as his master . . . Fear not them which kill the body . . .' (*Matt.* 10:16–28). These words are stern and honest. Those who first heard them must have felt they were a summons to quit all earthly ease. If men want heaven on easy terms they must re-write Christ's sermons. He gives us no prospect of a discipleship without trial or tribulation.

It would be wrong of us to read such words of Christ as if they referred only to the apostles or to biblical times. That such afflictions would be common to God's people in all ages is clear enough from the testimony of the New Testament as a whole. 'We must through much tribulation enter into the kingdom of God' (*Acts* 14:22). 'If the world hates you, ye know that it hated me before it hated you' (*John* 15:18). 'Beloved, think it not strange concerning the fiery trial which is to try you' (*1 Pet.* 4:12). 'These are they which came out of great tribulation' (*Rev.* 7:14). It is clear that the pathway to everlasting glory is one which in all ages and for all pilgrims has some experience of tribulation, of fiery trial and of this world's cruel hatred.

If such texts as the above had not been written we would stumble and be offended at the way God's people have been treated in this world. The history of Christ's church in some ages has been a veritable martyrology. It was often so in the Roman Empire before Constantine. It was often so in the Middle Ages. It was so at the Reformation and in Covenanting times. It is probably so still in Sudan, North Korea, parts of Indonesia and in some other areas of the world at this very hour. For all the centuries of Christian influence and missionary work, of Bible printing and distribution, of democratic governments and humanitarian enterprises, this world is still very much a scene of suffering to those who love Jesus Christ. The world is still the world and it will be the world ever until Christ comes to burn it with fire.

It is tempting to the Christian to want to live a life free from cares and problems here below, but it is not realistic. Even in lands where churches are well-established and where Christianity is socially acceptable, the believer must expect to find himself repeatedly buffeted and pilloried as he lives for Christ and witnesses to him. If the afflictions and the pains are less outward and more inward they are not the less real and lively to his experience. There is a cross to be carried which cannot be seen by any eye but God's. There is a fiery trial which must still be felt inwardly by the mind and soul. Even if it does not consume the body it may consume the heart. In our tolerant democracies where there is no martyr's bonfire there may be situations which roast God's people with fiery fears and stretch them on beds of nails. We are in the apostolic succession if we sometimes experience 'fightings without' and 'fears within' (*2 Cor.* 7:5).

A Christianity which attempts to live in cotton-wool is either compromised or, at best, cowardly. It might be just possible for a real Christian to avoid confrontation with this world by being as like it as he dare. But such a Christianity will not bring much glory to God or much reward to those who fashion themselves according to it. Where would truth be today had men not stood up in its defence at the cost of their lives? 'For this cause came I into the world, that I should bear witness unto the truth' (*John* 18:37). So said Christ to Pontius Pilate. 'Ye stiff-necked and uncircumcised in heart and ears!' (*Acts* 7:51). So cried the brave martyr Stephen before the corrupt Sanhedrin. 'Athanasius is against the world', cried that bold hero as he defended the divinity of Christ against the Arians. 'Here I stand!', exclaimed Luther as he pleaded before the church dignitaries at Worms for a return to the biblical gospel. These all suffered to give us our Bible and to keep open to view the door that leads to life.

To look for a gospel that involves us in no suffering is to desire an absurdity. The gospel which we preach is threatening. It threatens the kingdom of Satan. It threatens men's foolish love of sin. It threatens the way of life of *all* who are not already penitent and converted. Sinners know instinctively that the gospel requires of them nothing less than total surrender to the claims of Christ. To the worldly mind anything is better than to have to face up to a personal confrontation with an Almighty God. Anything, to the carnal mind, is a relief which does not challenge their conscience with the need to become holy. Since this is so, it cannot be otherwise for worldly men than that they must hate true Christians, who represent to them all that they would prefer not to know or to be.

To try to make Christianity painless is like trying to pretend that lions are harmless fun, or that dynamite is safe for children to play with. Pain lies at the very heart of Christianity. The whole life of Christ was painful and his death was exquisitely painful. The history of Christ's people, both Old Testament and New, is one of pain. Which great preacher had a pain-free life? Not Paul or Peter; not James or John; not Whitefield or Wesley; not Boston or the Erskines.

To expect to live the Christian life without any agony or anguish is to misunderstand the very essence of Christ's religion. A Christ without the nails and thorns is no Christ at all.

Too much modern Christianity is preoccupied with the subject of how to make life painless. Men seek gifts of healing, attend meetings for healing, study at classes where they can become healers. This healing-ministry emphasis is everywhere. But perhaps what we ought to be doing rather is to pray, not for the gift of healing, but for the gift of patience in suffering (*Rom.* 12:12). We need not so much meetings or conferences on healing as on courage to do our duty, boldness to live consistent lives, strength to put the claims of God before our own self-interest.

What a shallow thing our gospel would be if it gave painlessness to all believers! Do we forget in our comfortable modern life that pain, suffering, hunger and death are still staring people in the face in many parts of the world every day they live? Life in this world of sin is of necessity a sad, short and painful experience for multitudes. The Christian must go through his own share of all this sorrow. Sanctified afflictions are God's way of weaning us off the world and preparing us to leave it. Suffering teaches the Christian many lessons which he would never learn without it.

At the root of all this effort to anaesthetize the pain of Christian discipleship is almost certainly the false idea that 'God never wants his children to feel pain'. But such a view of God is foreign to the Bible, both Old Testament and New. God is aiming, not so much at the Christian's comfort here on earth, as at his holiness. Rest and comfort will belong to the believer eternally in a better world. They are not to be sought – at least, not to be sought *first* – in this present world. To put our own comfort first is to make an idol of this life. This is what the foolish do; God's children must not do so. Paul's earnest expectation should be ours: 'That Christ shall be magnified . . . whether it be by life, or by death' (*Phil.* 1:20).

The Christian and the Christian church are usually at their best in times of suffering. God-sent afflictions have a health-giving effect upon the believer's soul. They clear his eye-sight so that he recognises this world as the wicked, godless place that it is. Afflictions, when blessed by God, are the medicine used to purge the soul of its worldliness and its love of life's vanities. Those who have been in the crucible have lost more of their scum. They who have been in the fire with Christ have felt the sweetness of his presence, as few others have. When we are in trouble the promises of God's Word are more precious to us than gold. So, too, the church's suffering times are often her golden ages.

There will to the very end be trials in this life for God's people. Our ultimate comfort lies in this, that all Christ's promises will outlive this short life: 'In the world ye shall have tribulation: but be of good cheer; I have overcome the world' (*John* 16:33).

9

The Strife of Tongues

It is one of the welcome promises of God that he will hide his people 'from the strife of tongues' (*Psa.* 31:20). The phrase is a notable one: *strife* of tongues'. The tongues of sinners are never still but are forever battering against the reputations of others, especially against God's children. To live in this fallen world means to be in an arena of strife. Especially do those who dare to stand on the Lord's side need to expect to suffer the reproaches of others. The more a Christian lives for God, the more he will be a target for people to fire at with sharp and hurtful criticisms.

The Bible's theology of the human tongue is one to which we should pay careful heed if we mean to live on earth for God. There are passages of Scripture devoted specially to this theme of the fallen tongue. They bear out the same view as that above: the tongue is a weapon with which the sinful man and woman love to attack God's saints. They 'whet (or sharpen) their tongue like a sword' (*Psa.* 64:3). They 'bend their bows to shoot their arrows, even bitter words: that they may shoot in secret at the perfect: suddenly do they shoot at him and fear not' (*Psa.* 64:3–4). 'Thy tongue deviseth mischiefs; like a sharp razor, working deceitfully . . . Thou lovest all devouring words, O thou deceitful tongue' (*Psa.* 52:2, 4). 'The words of his mouth were smoother than butter, but war was in his heart: his words were softer than oil, yet were they drawn swords' (*Psa.* 55:21). This is the testimony of the Old Testament Scriptures. Even the most radical critic could not claim the Bible to be out of date on this point.

What we find in the Old is exactly matched by the teaching of the New Testament also. 'Those things which proceed out of the mouth come forth from the heart; and they defile the man. For out of the heart proceed evil thoughts . . . false witness, blasphemies' (*Matt.* 15:18–19). This is the explicit testimony of Christ, who 'knew what was in man'.

It is exactly echoed by the Apostle Paul: 'Their throat is an open sepulchre (or grave); with their tongues they have used deceit; the poison of asps is under their lips: whose mouth is full of cursing and bitterness' (*Rom.* 1:29–30). So much is this misuse of the tongue a part of our fallen society that those too who love Jesus Christ need to be exhorted to 'put away lying' and 'speak the truth' (*Eph.* 5:25). Even those who profess godliness must exert themselves to put to death all lying. In a famous passage of his Epistle, the writer James describes the true character of man's tongue. 'It is a little member, and boasteth great things . . . The tongue is a fire, a world of iniquity . . . it defileth the whole body, and setteth on fire the course of nature; and it is set on fire of hell' (*James* 3:5–6). The tongue is a match that can light a forest fire. The tongue that sings loud praise to God can next day damn our fellow-man. The tongue is as fiery and poisonous as it is uncontrollable. Nor should we suppose that the tongue will ever get better with the progress of time. 'In the last days . . . men shall be . . . boasters, proud, blasphemers . . . false accusers' (*2 Tim.* 3:1–3).

The gospel will civilize, educate and reform many evils. But while the world stands man's tongue will be what it has been since the Fall: 'lying and . . . deceitful' (*Psa.* 120:2). Its final punishment in unsaved men and women will be to have a judgment all of its own: 'What shall be given unto thee? Or what shall be done unto thee, thou false tongue? Sharp arrows of the mighty with coals of juniper' (*Psa.* 120:3–4). It would seem that the tongues of those in hell will burn with seven-fold intensity as a reward for their bitter cruelty in this life. We are told that they will there 'gnaw their tongues for pain' (*Rev.* 16:10).

To review, as we do above, the biblical teaching on the human tongue is to remind ourselves as believers that we are not to be surprised when the world or the false Christian speaks ill of us. It is precisely what it has ever done.

The hatred for God and for all his people can set the tongue of evil men all ablaze in a moment. How sadly we see this in the words which angry King Saul addresses even to his own son and heir, the godly Jonathan: 'Thou son of the perverse rebellious woman!' (*1 Sam.* 20:30). The words were as sharp-pointed as the javelin which was soon thrown after them at Jonathan. They belong to the same class as Shimei's words to David as he was fleeing from Absalom: 'Come out, come out, thou bloody man, and thou man of Belial!' (*2 Sam.* 16:7). Jonathan and David were men of as fine character as ever lived on earth, but both needed God's promise to screen them from the 'strife of tongues' and both were grateful for it in their day.

So too was our blessed Saviour Jesus Christ. Those who feel they have had more than their 'share' of verbal cruelty would do well to study again the bitter attacks made against the only perfect Man who was ever born into this world. He was subjected to a fierce battery of accusations which would have crushed most men. To his critics Christ was a sabbath-breaker (*Matt.* 12:2); he performed his miracles by the prince of the devils (*Matt.* 12:24); he (with his disciples) transgressed the tradition of the elders (*Matt.* 15:2). He was challenged as to the authority by which he ministered (*Matt.* 21:23); he was tempted by his enemies to say too much (*Matt.* 22:15); he was required to answer puzzling questions (*Matt.* 22:28) and repeatedly he was subjected to the attempts of hypocritical religious leaders to catch him out (*Matt.* 23).

Those faithful men who, for Christ's sake, are placed in similar circumstances would do well to recall that their Master himself suffered such encounters all through his ministry and is well able, now that he is in glory, to hide his people under a canopy from the 'strife of tongues'.

But this hatred towards Jesus Christ reached a crescendo when at last his critics had him on trial and on the Cross and could indulge their spleen without reserve or apology. On trial – ah! What a trial! – in the high priest's palace, our Lord's confession of Godhood was met with the words: 'He hath spoken blasphemy . . . behold, now ye have heard his blasphemy, what think ye?' To which the hoped-for answer was given, 'He is guilty of *death*' (*Matt.* 26:65–66).

Follow at this point our Saviour's cruel sufferings as they prepare him for his crucifixion and one thing becomes clear: there never was such a 'strife of tongues' as he suffered now from these religious men. 'Let him be crucified!'; 'His blood be on us, and on our children!'; 'Hail, King of the Jews!'; 'They that passed by reviled him, wagging their heads . . .'. 'If thou be the Son of God, come down . . . '. 'He saved others; himself he cannot save!' It is all written down in the twenty-seventh chapter of Matthew's Gospel and stands on record for ever, how sinful man accosted the Lord of glory himself with words of hateful spite and malice.

But in spite of all this cruel mockery and hatred, Christ had a 'pavilion' over his soul to protect him from all his detractors. He had knowledge and assurance which strengthened his innermost soul against all the cruel words shouted at him. So the Apostle Peter can write: 'When he was reviled, he reviled not again; when he suffered, he threatened not; but committed himself to him that judgeth righteously' (*1 Pet.* 2:23). Our Saviour turned, as it were, a deaf ear to the blood-thirsty ejaculations of his haters because he saw above and beyond them the righteous judgment of God, which would, in the course of time, both repay their cruelty and vindicate his own innocence.

This is therefore true also of every sincere follower of Christ. It is not, of course, true of believers, as it is true of Christ, that they are fully *innocent*. But it is equally true of them, as of him, that the judgment of God will vindicate them if they are suffering for well-doing and for Christ's sake. The same apostle puts the same 'pavilion' over the followers of Christ as he puts over Christ himself: 'For the eyes of the Lord are over the righteous and his ears are open unto their prayers: but the face of the Lord is against them that do evil' (*1 Pet.* 3:12). Christ, who suffered once for sins, has now 'gone into heaven' (*1 Pet.* 3:22) as his reward. And believers too will one day be raised up to be with the Lord. It was the reward given to Christ for his faithful and obedient suffering; it is the reward of grace to all who suffer similarly for the love they bear to Christ in this life.

The canopy of knowledge and understanding therefore which the Lord puts over his own people in times when they are subjected to reproaches, is sufficient to keep them from turning aside from the path of duty, even when they feel deeply hurt by lies and unjust accusations.

Christ felt the hurt of those bitter words which were hurled so unrighteously at him: 'Thou hast known my reproach, and my shame, and my dishonour: mine adversaries are all before thee. Reproach hath broken my heart . . . ' (*Psa.* 69:19–20). But, deeply as their words wounded our Lord's spirit, he rose above them and kept a wise devout silence: 'I have heard the slander of many . . . they devised to take away my life. But I trusted in thee, O Lord: I said, thou art my God. My times are in thy hand' (*Psa.* 31:13–15). So, again: 'I, as a deaf man, heard not' (*Psa.* 38:13).

There will be a sure reward to all who suffer unjust reproach for Christ's sake. The tables will be turned on all who unkindly injure and insult those who seek to live with a good conscience unto God: 'Let them be ashamed and brought to confusion together that rejoice at mine hurt:

Let them be clothed with shame and dishonour that magnify themselves against me' (*Psa.* 35:26).

Far different will be the portion of all who particularly bear the reproaches of those who wrongfully accuse them: 'Let them shout for joy, and be glad, that favour my (that is, Christ's) righteous cause' (*Psa.* 35:27).

Let every true believer seek refuge in this promise when he is tempted to answer back to those who revile him: 'Thou shalt keep them secretly in a pavilion from the strife of tongues' (*Psa.* 31:20).

Christ himself will have the last word to his own people: 'Come, ye blessed of my Father.'

THE LIFE OF GRACE
– THE FELLOWSHIP
OF THE CHURCH

10

The Duty of Mutual Submission

Among the varied duties set before the Christian in Scripture is that of mutual submission: 'Submitting yourselves one to another in the fear of God' (*Eph.* 5:21). Peter has the same exhortation: 'Likewise, ye younger, submit yourselves unto the elder. Yea, all of you be subject one to another' (*1 Pet.* 5:5). This is explained and amplified: 'Be clothed with humility; for God resisteth the proud, and giveth grace to the humble. Humble yourselves therefore under the mighty hand of God, that he may exalt you in due time' (verses 5–6). In point of good order, the wife is to submit to her own husband and the younger Christian to the elder, but as a matter of Christian love, *all* are to be submissive to one another. There can be no denying that this is how the New Testament addresses those who belong to Christ.

This grace of submissiveness is easy to overlook in the reading of the Bible. It is a duty which is seldom preached on and seldom referred to. Like many other exhortations of God's Word, it lies on the page of truth but is hastily skimmed over. The preacher's trawling eye does not consider it important enough to make it his text, nor does the Bible reader pay much heed to it. We miss the more modest duties of Scripture since we are in a hurry to scale the high mountains of elevated doctrine. But this we do to our loss and to the hurt of the church at large. How many churches have vanished because half their members would not submit to the other half! Doctrine they had, but not submission.

It is never a Christian's duty to submit to his brethren when they go wrong. The Bible knows of no charity which would promote peace at the expense of truth. An unprincipled unity built on some nebulous and creed-less consensus may be graced with the name of 'church', but it is not a church in the New Testament sense. Where there is no creed, there is no Christ. And where a church has no Christ, mutual submission is no better than a conspiracy to rob God of his honour.

A Christian who finds himself in a church situation where truth is not acted on must voice his strong protest. This is how the Old Testament prophets acted in days when the policies of godless kings and queens aimed at supression of true religion. This is how Christ acted when the visible church of his day was overspread with traditions and regulations contrary to Scripture. So did the apostles when they refused to obey the corrupt commands of the Sanhedrin.

The Christian's duty is never to submit in heart or conscience to what is contrary to the clear teaching of the Bible. Rather, he must 'obey God rather than men' (*Acts* 5:29). There is nowhere in the Bible any commandment to be silent when the church sets out on a course of sin and evil.

We submit to one another as Christians, whoever we are and whatever gifts we have, because we all have one and the same Master. This means that we differ from one another, whether we be young or old in the faith, only as brethren in the Lord. As brethren, gifted or not, we have something to share with one another which all can benefit from. The youngest believer, and the least gifted, has in his soul an experience of Christ's pardoning love, which is profitable for the most advanced saint to hear. Even the Apostle Paul at the height of his powers could speak of looking forward to 'being comforted by the mutual faith both of you and me' (*Rom.* 1:12). Evidently the apostles did not disdain the company or conversation of young converts.

God has given to us this duty of mutual submission to check ugly faults in our unsanctified natures. Nothing blows up our proud hearts so much as being elevated to some place of importance in the church. Not without cause has Satan been, through the centuries, an advocate of unscriptural offices in the church. High office produces, as a rule, high-mindedness. Even the biblical offices of elder and deacon are enough to elevate some professing Christians so high that they look down on lesser brethren as hardly worth listening to. It is to curb and cure this superior spirit that God bids all his people, the great as well as the small, to 'submit to one another'.

There is another good reason why Scripture bids us be subject one to another. It is that we might not be 'wise in our own eyes and prudent in our own sight' (*Isa.* 5:21). There are churches and fellowships which become so exclusive that they will have no fellowship with any but those of their own group. This is a regrettable and an unscriptural attitude to adopt. It is justified entirely to refuse to treat other churches as churches if they do not accept the sole authority of Scripture. But where other churches seek honestly to walk by the rule of Christ's Word, we are obliged to treat them as brethren and to have, at least, cordial and fraternal association. 'Salute every saint in Christ Jesus' (*Phil.* 4:21). 'Whereto we have already attained, let us walk by the same rule, let us mind the same thing' (*Phil.* 3:16).

The sad effect of having fellowship with none but our own group is that we unconsciously become convinced that 'we are the people and wisdom shall die with us' (*Job* 12:2). It is good to be made self-critical, lest we suppose ourselves above criticism. To mix only with those Christians who share our identical practice is to run the risk of not noticing that God gives excellent gifts also to those not of our group – and sometimes God gives *more* grace and usefulness to them. This is not to say that we should give up our good practice because gifted and good men do not share it. But it should send us back to God's Word to 'prove all things' (*1 Thess.* 5:21). Our best practice may, in some cases, be built on nothing more substantial than the venerable opinions of respected leaders and nothing more.

Hard as it is for our over-confident minds, it is good for us to meet with faithful men who are not of our group. It is good for us to be forced to test our beliefs and our practices. Where we are right we shall be the stronger; where wrong, we shall be obliged to reform. 'As iron sharpeneth iron', so brethren whose rule is Scripture will correct and refute one another by mutual converse and religious discussion. Even where we cannot adopt a brother's views or opinions as our own, we can submit ourselves to him to the extent that, respecting his sincerity, we permit ourselves to be influenced by him for good whenever possible.

If we are to submit to one another in the Lord, we shall have to learn to listen to one another in conversation. Fellowship is sharing and, in conversation, that means give and take. The art of conversation is to ask a few questions now and then, and to wait for an answer.

We submit to one another when we request their prayers. This the apostles did frequently. '[Pray] for me, that utterance may be given unto me' (*Eph.* 6:19). 'Brethren, pray for us' (*1 Thess.* 5:25).

We submit to one another when we 'confess our faults one to another' (*James* 5:16). In the course of the Middle Ages this formula was altered to mean that the layman should confess to the priest. But no such thought is intended in the New Testament. There are times when it is perfectly proper for the older, more experienced Christian to confess his shortcomings to the younger. The writer recalls once hearing a famous preacher confess his sorrow at not keeping a promise many years before. The obvious grief which this still brought to the venerable man's mind was a lesson for life. It emphasized the importance of keeping one's word better than ten sermons from some other preachers could have done.

Though the woman is not to preach or to take eldership in the church (*1 Cor.* 14:34, *1 Tim.* 2:11; 3:1–2), she can do excellent work in a private capacity, even in the realm of teaching doctrine. Apollos' advancement in gospel light came not only from conversation with Aquila but also with his wife, Priscilla (*Acts* 18:26). Spurgeon confessed he learned his theology from a cook! A cook who is sound in the faith is worthier of being a private tutor in Christian doctrine than a learned scholar who denies God's truth either by his lip or by his life.

It is quite proper for Christian men, whether ministers or not, to submit to listening to wise words from the lips of godly women in the context of a Christian group or gathering. Sometimes good women make a virtue of contributing nothing in company, when a choice word from them would be an ornament of gold in the eyes of those gathered for fellowship.

We submit to one another when we seek advice from one another. 'In the multitude of counsellors there is safety' (*Prov.* 11:14). Never make an important decision hastily – especially when you are tired or depressed. Rather, go to trusted friends in the Lord and seek their mind on important decisions. Of course, we are not to follow any man's advice uncritically. Take soundings from three or four if possible – then weigh the advice and pray for clear light. If in doubt, wait. Many a good man has blundered into a thicket of troubles for want of submitting to the kind counsel of wise friends. If we are not in a mood to take advice, we are in no fit state to take decisions. If only those men who resign hastily from the ministry would talk first with their real friends!

A wise man will listen to the rebuke of a faithful friend. 'Let the righteous smite me; it shall be a kindness: and let him reprove me; it shall be an excellent oil, which shall not break my head' (*Psa.* 141:5). The measure of our sanctification is the degree of our readiness to listen to a well-aimed rebuke. The truth hurts us because it *is* the truth about us. But grace teaches us to prefer being hurt with a good rebuke to being given over to our own wisdom. 'Thou art the man' (*2 Sam.* 12:7) hurt David like a sharp sword, but this bitter medicine was the remedy his soul needed. When Christians love one another they will at times need to rebuke one another. To such rebukes, when just and fair, we do well to submit, with thankfulness to God.

Love is very thin in any church or fellowship where a benign rebuke is badly taken. The rule is: 'Thou shalt in any wise rebuke thy neighbour, and not suffer sin upon him' (*Lev.* 19:17). The trouble with many of us is that we prefer a cowardly silence to giving a faithful admonition. The result is that all sorts of sins are tolerated which sadly mar the fair face of Christ's church.

I I

Dealing with Our Differences

Perfect harmony among God's people is not to be expected before we get to heaven. There, where all infirmity and all ignorance is over and gone forever, the Lord's people will 'see eye to eye' on everything. There all mysteries will be explained to all the saints, and all the controverted points of doctrine and duty will be made plain. There our present imbalances, obsessions, prejudices, and other imperfections will be behind us. Truth will shine bright upon every redeemed mind, and every saint will embrace every other with consummated affection and delight. Not the least shadow of division will cloud the unity of the church in her state of coming glory. 'Ephraim shall not envy Judah, and Judah shall not vex Ephraim' (*Isa.* 11:13). But we shall be 'one' (*John* 17:21) as the three everblessed Persons of the glorious Godhead are 'one', in harmony, truth and love.

That such harmony does not exist yet among God's people is no surprise. There are various factors at work which make it difficult for them to see 'eye to eye' now as they will in their future state.

For one thing 'we know in part, and we prophesy in part' (*1 Cor.* 13:9). Our understanding of God's will is very far from perfect here below. This is true not only among those whose doctrine of Scripture is defective. It is true, at least in measure, even among those who sincerely believe the Bible to be 'the only rule to direct us' how to glorify and enjoy God. Try as we may to understand them, there are texts of Scripture whose true sense and meaning eludes us. Study as we may, there are aspects of doctrine and practice which God's people cannot yet agree fully on.

A second reason for this partial disunity among those who truly love God arises from the differences of temperament among them. It is not an easy thing to say precisely what lies behind the difference in men's temperaments. But, whether the difference be the fruit of nature or nurture, one of gifts or of graces, whether it be entirely the result of sin or entirely of God's providence, this difference between men, even the best of men, is often very great and leads to their adopting different views of the truth and of their duty in relation to it. For this reason the best of Christians, who in other respects are one in their love for God and truth, may sometimes diverge sharply from one another till they even take up public positions against one another.

Yet another explanation for our differences as God's people in this life arises from the different degrees of sanctification among us. In all probability, among those who are sound in their grasp of Christian doctrine, this factor is the strongest, especially in our 'domestic' disputes. Our failures to mortify self-love, our fallen affections, our natural jealousies, our enjoyment of position and reputation, our lack of meekness and a thousand similar flaws of sanctification lead us to make more of our differences than we should.

How hard it can be to 'esteem others better than ourselves' (*Phil.* 2:3)! How hard it can be to overcome our prejudices, to alter our own opinionated ways of doing the work of God, to believe that others may have more light on a truth than we have and therefore more right to be listened to than ourselves!

A healthy recognition of the fact that sin has ruined us all more than we realize would go a long way towards softening disputes between brethren! It is the proof of Christian greatness when a man can admit that he was formerly in the wrong, as Augustine did when he wrote his *Retractations*.

Let it be stated emphatically that the worst course of action possible among Christians would be to sink all our differences under a misguided belief that unity is the most important thing of all. Unity without truth is a unity under the headship of Satan, not of Christ. Whatever the supposed evils of division among believers, they are a thousand times more to be desired than indifference to doctrine. Truth is sacred. It is more precious than life. Its claims are greater than all other claims.

A man must die, if necessary, in defence of the truth. But it would hardly be his duty to die for unity. To lose unity among Christians in this life is inconvenient and may, in some circumstances, be sinful. But to lose truth is to lose God, heaven and the gospel itself. If truth is lost, all that matters is lost. If unity is lost, it is lost only for a time. It will be restored to God's people eventually, either here or hereafter.

The division which exists in Christendom between those who hold to central truths and those who do not must always be a most welcome division. It may suit the poetic tastes of some romantic churchmen to preach about the 'wounds in the body of Christ's church caused by lack of outward unity'. But it is mere superstitious cant if all that is meant by it is that evangelicals will not join a doctrinally corrupt ecumenism. Churches, however old and venerable, if they do not hold to the basic doctrines of the Word of God, are not true churches at all but only 'synagogues of Satan' (*Rev.* 3:9). It is every true Christian's duty to refuse church fellowship to those who deny the cardinal truths of Scripture or else affirm as central truths things which Scripture does not so affirm.

The truth of the gospel may be destroyed in either of two ways. It is destroyed when churches deny central truths such as the atonement of Christ or the doctrine of justification by faith. Alternatively, the gospel is destroyed when a church affirms central doctrines in theory but at the same time denies in its practice the things implied by those central doctrines. For instance, a church might have a true doctrine of justification in its denominational creed but might tolerate the practice of saying masses and allowing auricular confession among its clergy. The toleration of the latter destroys the force of the former.

Or again, a church might profess an orthodox creed but destroy itself by refusing to exercise righteous discipline among its members. This practical evil is destructive of the theoretical soundness of the church. Given time, the creed too will be altered. Truth always has powerful implications.

It is rightly intolerant of all that threatens it, whether in theory or in practice.

What has just been stated here illustrates that not all divisions among Christians are vicious. They are virtuous, and indeed essential, if the division exists to preserve the truth of the gospel. Not for nothing does the New Testament warn us: 'Have no fellowship with the unfruitful works of darkness but rather reprove them' (*Eph.* 5:11). Not without good reason does the Apostle Paul state: 'Of your own selves shall men arise, speaking perverse things, to draw away disciples after them' (*Acts* 20:30). For a sound church to contemplate having any official fellowship or association with an unsound church is treason to Jesus Christ and to the souls of God's people in the congregation.

However, not all the divisions and differences which arise among the people of God are so simple to deal with as the obvious difference between truth and error. Sadly, there are painful divisions between excellent men who hold substantially, if not indeed precisely, to the same creeds and confessions. The question must be faced, How are Christians to deal with these more sensitive differences?

Believing as we must do that differences among sound Christians are regrettable and that steps should be taken to repair torn relationships, we would suggest that the following are useful practical measures to that end:

1. It should be a rule among God's people *to be ready to recognize excellence* wherever we find it and to be prepared to learn from one another even when, in some secondary matters, we may have to differ from one another. To state this is to imply that men may be better than their creed.

Those whose views on some matters we may disagree with may nonetheless have much to teach us on some other Christian virtue.

2. It would be a help if brethren who hold to the truths of orthodoxy with some rather strong distinctives of their own would *refrain from stating those distinctives too often or too loudly*. Beyond a certain point of common biblical agreement there are views of doctrine which good men may choose to hold or not, according as they are persuaded. The temptation is that some men feel conscience bound to crusade for their *shades of opinion*. Overlooking the ninety-eight per cent of agreement held in common with good men almost everywhere we can develop a mentality of striving always over that small fraction of truth which is peculiar to our own group. Whatever the point of doctrine at issue, this has been a source of needless division and dissension all through history.

3. It would be a healthy exercise for ministers and elders who are in 'dogmatic' denominations *to attend conferences* where they can regularly meet faithful men who are not of their own group. There are several advantages to this. In small denominations especially, good people are apt to fall into bad habits of thought and speech. It is a snare to suppose that '*our* group is the best in the world' or that '*our* way of doing it is the right way and all others need to learn from *us*'. Such attitudes may not always be put into words but they often secretly exist in good men's minds. To go to conferences where other excellent men meet and debate areas of truth can be humbling for us. In the context of a wider fellowship we are to examine our own cherished opinions and compelled to

recognize that God gives outstanding gifts to men in circles other than our own. Truth does not begin and end with any one church or denomination, however good.

4. It is wise in our estimation of doctrines, ministers and churches to *leave room for surprises*. The strange truth is that those with whom we are in vigorous agreement today may be those with whom we shall strenuously disagree tomorrow. In the life of all churches it frequently happens that men alter their position and change their ground.

Today's apostle for the 'signs and wonders' movement may prove to be tomorrow's staunchest preacher of 'orthodoxy', and today's pulpit hero may be tomorrow's traitor to Christ's cause. Those who come new to the doctrines of grace may be those who in the end will have loved and promoted them best; and those who were brought up in orthodox manses and in orthodox families may end up, like Esau, despising their spiritual birthright. If we know these things we shall not make too much of 'our party' or of 'our circle' but be ready to value sincere love of truth even if presently tinged with some immaturity and ignorance.

5. If we are to manage our differences as Christians we need to guard against *becoming wise in our own eyes*. The devil is never more an angel of light than when he urges us to be ever stronger and more adamant in our own ideas. To hold to the truth is excellent. But there is such a thing as straining a doctrine beyond its biblical proportions till, unwittingly, we have distorted a gospel truth to the point where it is scarcely recognizable. We may stress piety till it becomes pietism; or preparation till it becomes preparationism; or liberty till it becomes licence; or law till it becomes legalism;

or faith till it is no better than the faith of devils (*James* 2:19). In doctrine, as in matters of practical duty, it is possible to forget that 'overdoing leads to undoing'.

6. If we are to avoid needless division let us *make most of those great central truths* which are acknowledged and loved by all the people of God. When we meet in a fellowship-meeting a brother in Christ who happens to differ from us in some particular, do we need to challenge him on his opinion or should we speak about matters on which we both agree? Some believers evidently feel that their duty is to overlook all that is held in common with the brother and to attempt at once to 'put him right'. It is not easy to lay down absolute rules, of course, but experience suggests that much of the time which men are apt to spend in controversy over lesser matters would be better spent on the great central themes. Our deepest need is to grow in the knowledge and love of Christ himself. This being so, why should we not in our times of fellowship direct our discussions towards such questions as these:

How can we seek a richer experience of Christ's love? By what means can we best show our love to Christ? How can we better bear one another's burdens and so fulfil the law of Christ? How can we best prepare to give a good account to Christ when we stand before him? What means have we found most helpful in rousing our feelings of gratitude to Christ?

There is much good to be gained by our differences as Christians. Every one in the fellowship of God's people has something valuable to offer. Each one has some 'measure of the gift of Christ' (*Eph.* 4:7). The many-sided wisdom of God is made clear to us in the way the people of God are all so different in the measure of their gifts, graces and knowledge. It is a thousand pities when these differences become the occasion of alienating brethren from one another. This can happen all too easily when we ride roughshod over one another in discussion, debate and conversation. It can happen, too, when doubtful opinions are reckoned as dogmas and minor matters contended for as if the very life of the gospel depended on them.

In such an atmosphere is it surprising if divisions have sometimes flourished; if animosities between brethren have sprung up like a thorn-hedge; if denominational walls a yard thick have been built to keep equally good men apart when they really belong together? The problem is an age-old one which goes back to the church's earliest days. No better solution two thousand years on in time can be found than they found all those years ago! 'In things essential, unity; in things not essential, liberty; in all things, charity.'

12

The Minister's Wife

Not many ministers' wives begin their married life by marrying a minister. Most of them marry a husband who is in secular employment and who enters the ministry only later in life. This is a fact which deserves to be mentioned because the minister's wife is often taken for granted and her many acts of service to a congregation can be received as children take their mother's love – with hardly a thought for the kindness behind it. A man enters the ministry out of a sense of call; but many a wife enters on the work of becoming the lady of the manse with misgivings and trepidation, led into the work because the man she has married has felt led into the work rather than because she feels any personal adequacy for it herself.

A minister sometimes receives honour and recognition for the work he does, but a minister's wife can easily be overlooked. Yet, if the congregation did but know it, their minister's wife is as much in the work and as much involved in its joys and sorrows as her husband is. *His* name alone appears in the Church Notices and in the advertisements placed in the local paper. But his wife, all unobserved by others, is silently, yet most importantly, upholding her husband in every aspect of his work for Christ and is therefore as much deserving of love and respect as he is.

The role of being a minister's wife must be one of the most taxing that any woman could have. To the many duties of wifehood and (probably) motherhood she has to add those of being a hostess, typist, secretary, Sabbath-school teacher and confidante. Her home is an office, library, committee-hall, Bible study venue, rendezvous for holiday friends and a sanctuary for prayer. She must add to her many accomplishments the art of exercising a prudent economy so that in her practised hands one pound can do the work of two. She is sweetness itself to all who cross her path (even to her husband's critics) and she remembers always to have the 'law of kindness' in her mouth (*Prov.* 31:26).

The minister's wife labours under 'disadvantages' which her husband does not have. *He* is in the public eye; *she* is not very often mentioned. *He* is always busy; *she* 'has nothing to do but tidy the manse' – or so it is commonly thought! What no eye outside the manse sees are the many ways in which she sustains her husband in every aspect of his ministry. Her ambition is not to be important in people's eyes but to keep her husband in his work. Few realize the ministry that God has given her and few notice how carefully she does it. But her great task is to keep her husband in the pulpit.

The minister's wife is the mother of the manse children. 'Manse children', at least in the judgment of some, are a special sort of children who are expected to be exemplary. This expectation is a good and right one, for if the minister 'know not how to rule his own house', he has no business ruling in God's house (*1 Tim.* 3:5). But since the minister himself is so busy, the bringing up of their children is very much left to the *lady* of the manse.

A minister's children often grow up without him noticing it! His work is so absorbing that the years of their childhood fly by and he only realizes when they are in their teenage years that they are not little children any longer, but now little adults. These years had to be supervised by someone other than the minister and, in the absence of anyone else to do it, they were supervised by his wife.

Every wife shares in the joys and sorrows of her husband and is a partaker of his losses or gains. So in an especial way is the minister's wife. She, more than most, knows by instinct when her husband is worried by problems. A congregation can be a place of pain as well as of pleasure and the pastor's face, which conceals from all others the inward agony he feels, is a well-read book to his sympathetic spouse. She marks his foreboding as he leaves to go to that dreaded church-meeting. She meets him at the door as he returns from what she knows must have been an excruciating experience as he faced the angry opposition of unreasonable men, who ought to have known better.

But these trying times pass by. God gives good times as well as sad times. Times of joy in a manse are truly times of heaven on earth for the minister and his faithful wife. 'A new convert, my dear!', he cries as he throws open the door of his sitting-room. 'The son of Deacon so-and-so was melted to tears under the Word of God tonight. He has given his life to God. Oh, blessed be God for his grace and goodness!'

Such news is heard in a manse from time to time and it is balm to the soul of both the minister and his wife. No joy is so rich in all this world as to see the dewy tear in the eye of one who has just found peace through the blood of Christ. Faithful pastors see it still and in this happy privilege their wives are joyful partakers.

A minister's wife does not know how long she will live in the house which she occupies. By faith she comes to a congregation, and by faith she stays there, serving her church and her family, often in a house that is not hers. At the back of her mind she has the thought that one day, any day, she may have to move her family and her furniture to another house – and perhaps to another and another after that.

When, often with startling suddenness, her husband is placed under 'call' to another church, she has to review all her plans and to revise all her domestic arrangements. She bids a sorrowful farewell to those dear people of God in the congregation whom she has now come to know so well. At last the thousands of books and the manse furniture are all packed in cartons and boxes. The removal van is at the door. Soon the place which she has loved for ten years will be little more than a memory and a matter of prayer.

No part of her work is harder to the minister's wife than to criticize her own husband's preaching. Yet at times she must do even this. 'Faithful are the wounds of a friend' (*Prov.* 27:6) and she knows that there are times when she must, for love's sake, tell her husband that he is going wrong in one way or another. 'My dear, you have preached four sermons in the last four weeks on the very same theme. Don't you think we should have a little variation?' Or, it may be: 'My dear, you are becoming so deep and so complex that not one in ten can follow you.' Or, again, 'My dear, you are forgetting the unconverted in the congregation. You *do* need to speak to their consciences more.' Usually, a minister can take criticism tolerably well from another minister. But it is the *really* sanctified preacher who can bear to be corrected by a lady – even the lady by his side. The pastor's wife knows this all too well. But she knows too that she *must* risk everything to ensure that her husband does not fall into some bad habit in his preaching. The preacher who goes off at tangents or who rides a hobby-horse is in need of a quiet 'aside' from his wife. It can be a painful experience for both parties, but one which yields good fruits to all concerned.

The minister's work is a physically and emotionally draining one and it belongs to his wife's experience to see him sometimes exhausted and brought almost to a standstill. Some days she has to give up her hope of a 'day-off' while he sleeps to recover himself. Other days she has to steel herself to the thought that her beloved husband must be 'handled with care' till he recovers from a period of special strain or unusual fatigue. In patience and with a wife's love she shares his burdens and so halves them for him. It is a ministry which very few see in this life but one which will be rewarded by an all-seeing Saviour when he comes.

Who can estimate the worth of a good lady of the manse? 'Her price is far above rubies' (*Prov.* 31:10). She may not receive her recognition in this life but she will get it in the next. Her ministry in this world is to minister to Christ's servant. It is her joy and calling to support a husband who is dedicated to the preaching of God's Word in this life. It is the honour of congregations to honour those who do the difficult work which God has given her to do.

If, after long years of service, she sees her once-youthful husband now slow and labouring in his duties, she has the comfort of knowing that she and he together will before long enter into their everlasting rest and reward. Even if she is called on to see him sicken and fall into the grave, she remembers that for him and for her death is but the doorway to glory and to Christ. 'Give her of the fruit of her hands; and let her own works praise her in the gates' (*Prov.* 31:31).

13

'In the Time of Old Age'

There are problems and cares which relate specially to the Christian 'in the time of old age' (*Psa.* 71:9); consequently, there are prayers and promises in God's Word which are specially given to help the believer as he approaches the end of his pilgrimage. The Bible is a handbook for saints and sinners at all stages of life. It is designed by God to be of comfort and help to us from the cradle to the grave. There is no situation for which the Bible offers no advice or brings no guidance. The people of God therefore need to live by faith in God's Word as much at the end of life as in youth and middle-age.

It is clear at a glance that Psalm 71 is one of the passages addressed to ageing saints. It has indeed been called *'The Old Man's Psalm'*. The expressions found in Psalm 71 are those of a saint nearing his end in this world: 'Thou art my trust from my youth' (v. 5); 'by thee have I been holden up from the womb' (v. 6); 'cast me not off in the time of old age' (v. 9); 'now also when I am old and grey-headed, O God, forsake me not; until I have shewed thy strength unto this generation' (v. 18). All such references in this Psalm indicate that it is designed to be of special help to the Lord's people when they near the age of seventy – or else have passed it.

There is a need for us to minister in these days to ageing saints. It is all too possible for them to be overlooked because of the emphasis upon youth in modern society.

In many churches there are old Christians who need to be helped and cared for with more than ordinary compassion. For one thing, old Christians are often rather confused and bewildered by all the changes which have occurred in society during their life-time. The twentieth century saw more changes than probably any century in human history, at least since the Flood. The tempo of life at the beginning of that century was much as it had been for centuries: horses and carts, a simple life-style and clearly understood codes for conduct, work, social standing and dress.

By the 1960s, and onwards, all earlier conventions were thrown to the four winds. In family, church and state, in the work-place and in the home, society was propelled into a whirlwind of new values. The tempo of life has changed, probably for ever, in the last fifty years. With change has come revolt against all that is 'old'. The 'old' are hardly wanted in the work-place any longer. Indeed, many of them are evidently not wanted in their own family circle any more. It is not therefore surprising that they can even feel unwanted in the very church where they have been worshippers for over half a life-time.

The elderly Christian may be neglected by the new, young minister quite unintentionally. It is understandable that he should have an eye to the good of the congregation in years to come. 'We must get young people in.' Every minister understands this problem today, when young people are generally everywhere else, but not in God's house. However, in a church climate where concern for 'youth' is always kept at fever-pitch, it is understandable that many of the best and most faithful church members feel like second-class citizens because they are now elderly, and overlooked.

If we could for a month or two become the proverbial fly on the wall of our evangelical churches throughout the nation, we strongly suspect that we should become conscious of a disproportionate interest in 'youth' work. At least, we would come to see more clearly that we have a pastoral duty to the elderly as well as to the young. It ought not, of course, to be either/or but both/and. Let zeal to evangelize the young go hand-in-hand with affectionate care for the mature saints. To neglect their good advice is to repeat the folly of Rehoboam, whose headstrong conduct brought tragic division among God's people (*1 Kings* 12). This cautionary example has not always been sufficiently heeded.

If we are to begin to minister to God's people 'in the time of old age' we must attempt to understand their special needs. For one thing, we must appreciate the excellent qualities of older Christians. Many of them have borne a quiet and steady testimony to Christ for half a century and more.

They prayed for the nation when Churchill called for national effort amid 'blood, toil, tears and sweat'. They prayed and trusted while Hitler's planes flew overhead and his rockets ruined our historic landmarks. They were in arms in the Middle East, in North Africa, in France when the Allied forces marched northwards to victory. They have painful memories which the young have scarcely dreamed of; they have gone through experiences in their youth which modern youth know only from history books. The elderly deserve our respect, love and gratitude not least for the sacrifices which they made to give us our modern peace and plenty. This gratitude is not always sufficiently visible, even among those who go to God's house.

Any preacher who goes round the churches in our land must soon become aware that it is often older Christians who are bearing the burden of God's work. It is they who do the lion's share of the practical service needed in many congregations. It is they who are conspicuously present each week at the Prayer Meeting. It is they who visit the hospital and the Old People's Home. Their lives are often the most consistently devoted to Christ. No doubt too their prayers are one of the great reasons why the judgment of God has not yet fallen upon our land so much as we deserve. Woe betide this country when their prayers and their persons are gone!

Our argument here, of course, is not that less be done for the young but that care be exercised in case our best and most spiritual people should be unintentionally overlooked. In practice this must mean that all changes in the conduct of worship and in the character of congregational life should consult the needs of the elderly as well as those of others.

What are the special fears and cares of old saints 'in the time of old age'? Some fear lest they be 'cast off' and 'forsaken by God' (*Psa.* 71:9). Strange as it may seem, old saints, perhaps because of the decay of their physical powers, may be troubled with fears that God will at last reject them.

It should help us to minister the more tenderly to them in this infirmity when we recall that we too may, in old age, be similarly tempted. As we preach to and visit them, let us remind them of the rich promises of God to all who persevere. 'Hearken unto me, O house of Jacob, and all the remnant of the house of Israel, which are borne by me from the belly, which are carried from the womb: And even to your old age I am he; and even to hoar hairs will I carry you: I have made, and I will bear; even I will carry, and will deliver you' (*Isa.* 46:3–4).

A common fear of old Christians is that they are a 'nuisance' to others, needing to be offered a helping hand wherever they go and requiring a 'lift' by car from someone. Their sense of being a burden to others is increased by the fact that they are probably hard of hearing and need to have things repeated to them. Elderly persons are usually sensitive to the fact that others must 'put up' with their many infirmities. The danger is that they develop a death-wish which others do not appreciate. It is good to desire to 'depart and be with Christ', but we must not allow the elderly to wish to 'go' because they think we do not understand them or because we appear to have no time to show them a little extra patience.

It scarcely needs to be said that the elderly Christian's thoughts are frequently of the past. His weakening constitution tells him that before too long his Master will summon him to quit his present 'house' and appear in another abode. The old saint has a full book of memories. The photographs on the sideboard and above the hearth are a poignant reminder to him of loved ones now 'gone'. The young do not yet know the thoughts that arise in the mind of the aged at the sight of an empty chair, or at the silence of an empty house where once were heard the lively shouts and tears of children now grown and gone away.

Let not one suppose the elderly have no foes to fear. It is one of the surprises of this *'Old Man's Psalm'* that David (as we suppose the author to be) had still his 'enemies'. It seems strange that an old king should need to pray, 'Deliver me, O my God, out of the hand of the wicked, out of the hand of the unrighteous and cruel man' (*Psa.* 71:4). Strange too that he still needs to cry, 'Mine enemies speak against me; and they that lay wait for my soul take counsel together' (v. 10).

In old age David still had an Absalom to vex him. And many an aged pilgrim of Christ has to pray still for 'deliverance' from 'foes', perhaps 'those of his own household', who do not share his or her love of the Saviour. Not a few ministers of the gospel have to visit elderly patients who are martyrs to the noisy, insensitive programmes listened to and watched by the family in the very room where the elderly must seek grace to bear what to a spiritual soul must be almost unbearable.

We must not forget that the elderly believer has a shadow over his mind which younger believers may not begin to realize: the seriousness of dying and facing God. It is true that the believer need fear no hurt in death. But only a fool forgets that death is still an 'enemy'. Death is a most serious event and must be prepared for. At the end the devil may put forth more power to darken the believer's mind and cloud his hope. It has happened to the best of saints. Their last days have included hours of conflict with dark fears, doubt and the dread that 'they were never truly converted'. Let those who question the accuracy of this reach for the great biographies on their bookshelf.

Younger Christians, especially in the ministry, would be sinning against Christ if they were to neglect the souls of elderly believers who look to them for some words of occasional encouragement, and receive none. It is not the advice of trained counsellors that old saints need but the gracious promises of Christ, read to them from the old Book by a loving friend. This ministry is a simple one. But it is sublime because done to Christ's veterans, and therefore, in His reckoning, done to Him. This is a ministry that no Christian ought to shun.

At every stage of a Christian's life there is God's promise of sufficient grace. At the closing stage of life, when our powers fail and even 'the grasshopper becomes a burden' (*Eccles.* 12:5) the child of God wants to hear talk only about one thing: a Saviour's love and rich mercy to sinners. No saint dies comfortably because he has done this or that for Christ. Our comfort in dying is that mercy is offered to 'the chief of sinners' (*1 Tim.* 1:15). Hypocrites may float along the stream towards the cataract of death with vain expectations of having 'merited' a bright future beyond the grave. But real Christians, even the very best, approach death with no merit in their eye except that of a blessed Saviour.

When we feel the grip of our 'last enemy' laid on our arm we must find strength nowhere but in the agony and blood of the Son of God. True saints know this. At the end they want to have it said to them a hundred times over by all who visit their sick-bed: 'The blood of Jesus Christ, God's Son, cleanseth us from all sin' (*1 John* 1:7).

'In the time of old age' the believer completes his service to God and puts the lid on the treasure which he has laid up in heaven. Now he can say: 'I have fought a good fight, I have finished my course, I have kept the faith' (*1 Tim.* 4:7). It is his joy now to be near to his everlasting rest. Soon he will put off his armour and put on robes of light. He will shortly sup with his Master in the beatific presence of God the Father and in the company of saints and angels. He leaves a world of curses and cares to enter a world of blessing, glory and love. The day of his death is better than that of his birth (*Eccles.* 7:1). The aged saint will shortly be discharged from the ranks of the church militant, in order to enjoy the company of the church triumphant who 'walk with Christ in white' (*Rev.* 3:4).

God grant us to be among them at the last!

14

Why Christians Must Be Readers[1]

The cloke that I left at Troas with Carpus, when thou comest, bring with thee, and the books, but especially the parchments (2 Tim. 4:13).

Paul is in prison and in a short time is to lose his life at the instigation of the Roman Emperor Nero. But in prison he invites Timothy to bring with him books and parchments. It is a most interesting scene. Here is a great man, full of the Spirit of God, with a life of fruitfulness almost unparalleled in the history of mankind. Soon he will leave this world and go to be with Christ. But in his prison cell he longs for something which Timothy can bring – books and parchments.

We cannot know for sure what these books and parchments were. They might, of course, have been the Scriptures of the Old Testament. We bear in mind that the New Testament Scriptures were only beginning to exist at this time as a collection of books. They certainly were not

[1] Taken from an address given to mark the twenty-eighth anniversary of the Reformation Book Centre, Adelaide, Australia, in 1997.

yet put together in the form of a completed New Testament. So in all likelihood these books and parchments included the Old Testament Scriptures. But Paul was a prolific reader and an indefatigable student. It is probable that amongst these books and parchments were other books, perhaps commentaries on Scripture or even secular books written by Greek writers of the pagan world. On two or three occasions Paul reveals his familiarity with pagan Greek literature. He evidently did not despise the best of the Greek literature.

At this point we might ask a question of our text. If it was the Bible of the Old Testament that Paul was asking to be brought, my question would be, 'Why did he need it?'. He had a consummately good memory. He had studied the Scriptures from his childhood, and he must have been almost able to quote the Old Testament from memory. Some people have achieved something similar. Why then would he need the Scriptures, if he had them stored away in his own mind?

On the other hand, if it was not the Bible of the Old Testament he was asking for, but other books, one might ask, 'Why would he want them?' He was, after all, so close to death and to glory. Soon he would see his Saviour's face and receive his immortal honours from Christ. You would hardly think that such a man would be interested to read anything but divine, spiritual and inspired literature. But whatever it was he wanted, and whatever it was he needed, he asked for these books to come. So we are faced with the question: Why?

Let me suggest three reasons.

First, I would suggest that if a man is once a reader, he is always a reader. And a prison cell to a reader becomes a home from home when there are books. A small shelf of familiar books is like a small cluster of familiar friends. How the apostle in prison at Rome would have rejoiced to see these old 'companions' beside him!

And then, as a second reason, it does not matter how advanced a Christian is in knowledge, grace, wisdom and experience; in this life he has not yet come to perfection. The apostle was forever pressing on to that perfection which was his desired goal.

Even as the shadow of eternity fell upon him, he was anxious that his dying days should be also learning days and days of progression. Evidently there were still things he had to learn, and he was humble enough to indicate his readiness to learn from books.

Let me offer to you a third reason. I would suggest that the apostle includes these words for Timothy's sake, as though to say to Timothy, 'You must be a reader, Timothy. You are taking up the work that I am laying down.'

Technically, Timothy was what we call an evangelist. An evangelist in the New Testament sense is what we would call an apostolic helper. He did not have plenary divine inspiration as the apostles did. Whenever the apostles opened their mouth officially to preach, what they said was infallible, conveying the very Word of God. But Timothy did not have that gift. His work was the consolidation of the churches of Christ, and it was essential that amongst other responsibilities that Timothy would take upon himself was reading the best books.

So I do not think it is straining the passage to say that the doctrine from these words is surely this: A Christian man or woman must be a reader, all his or her life. We are to be readers to our dying day.

No book is remotely comparable to the Bible. So it is most important that in talking about books we say something first about the way to read the Bible to greatest profit. When we read the Word of God, I believe we should try to memorize it and learn it off by heart. We cannot know the Bible too well.

We know nothing compared to some of our forefathers in the faith. Take the Waldensians. They were the evangelicals of the Middle Ages. They lived in northern Italy in remote and inaccessible valleys and hillsides. They maintained the Word of God in its integrity and purity for centuries. Their ministers more or less had to learn the New Testament by heart before they entered the ministry, and often they knew the Psalms also. We know our Bible so little compared with them. We are humbled to compare ourselves with them. The Waldensians are an inspiration to us to learn our Bible. It is not enough just to read it. We are to imbibe it until, like John Bunyan, our very blood is 'bibline' and the mind of Christ fills our whole conception of everything. Judge of everything by this book. That is the way in which we are to use the Bible.

Then, let me say, read the Bible so as to consolidate your theology. What is missing in many Bible readers today in the world is that they have not understood the theology of the Bible, and that is an incalculable loss. What is the theology of the Bible? It is the distillation of all its teachings. Put the

Bible in the crucible, heat it up, distill it to its essence, and what you have is what the world has learned to call 'Calvinism'.

The system of theology of the Bible is the system of grace which is enshrined for us in the Westminster Confession and Catechisms, and in similar statements of religious doctrine and belief. We must see that and have that consolidated more and more in our minds.

You will forgive me for being a little parochial if I say that there is one very good thing in the Highlands of Scotland that we could export to Christians all around the world. After the evening services and prayer meetings on a week-night and on the Lord's Day they frequently gather together in one or other of the homes of the congregation to talk about the Word of God. One of the men, let us say, will ask the questions, and another of the men will volunteer answers; and then other people will be drawn in to speak from their own experience about things relating to the text of Scripture that is being discussed.

God did not make us to be mindless. We begin with the mind. True religion begins with the mind, and that is what is so wonderful about Calvin, the Puritans, and those who followed on in the same linear succession. They begin with the mind. They address the mind. They give factual, propositional instruction to the intellect of man.

Then the Puritans addressed the heart. The mind is the first thing, but not the only thing. What we believe must affect our emotions, and that is what they believed in: the religion of the heart. Their books deal with such subjects as keeping the heart, and watching the heart, and resisting the devil and temptation. This is the practice of the Christian life. They dealt with every aspect of the believer's life: prayer; meditation; how to listen to sermons; how to sanctify the Sabbath day; our conduct in divine worship; family worship; the instruction of children; the Christian's daily walk and conversation; knowing your adversary the devil and his wiles.

Between the two world wars, Puritan books were worth next to nothing in England. You could go to a secondhand book dealer and ask for these books, and if there were any there to be had you could get them for maybe a shilling a volume. Nobody wanted them. They were simply being thrown out. Indeed, during the wartime they were being pulped by the government. You would receive a shilling or something for every ton of books that you turned in to some government agency, and they just pulped them for the war effort.

So thousands of the best theological books vanished in that way. But in 1957 a small start was made to reprint some of these great old books. You may know some of the early books that were published by the Banner of Truth Trust. When some of us who were young Christians in that period (as I was) started to read these books, it was like beholding a lost continent! It was like standing on the edge of a new world!

The Banner continued its work, and the work grew. When they first began to publish Puritans and to reprint Spurgeon, some Christian publishers said, with a smile, 'It's a waste of time, because nobody is going to buy these old books!' But they did, until it literally came to the stage that the demand for some of the books they published outstripped the supply. They could not get them out fast enough.

Some of these books are the very best books the world has ever seen. Scarcely any language in the world has had such books as the English language. Today if you go to countries which are influenced by the gospel, the first thing these other countries have to do is to read our language. In Korea today, and in other countries, Christians are learning our language because they want access to the Puritans!

I was very touched recently while in Korea to meet a number of young people who said to me, 'We have started a Puritan club.'

I said, 'What's that?'

'We get together and one of us reads from one of the Puritans to all the rest', (translated into Korean, of course).

I thought, What an extraordinary thing! Young people gathering to read the Puritans. But you see, my point is this: You and I don't need to learn the English language. We have it; we were born with it. It is our mother tongue. Shame on you and me if, having the language and having the books and having the means of getting them, we do not fill ourselves with this divine knowledge. Through reading the Word of God and the best books, the smell of heaven should be felt by others to be in our hearts and homes.

THE LIFE OF GRACE
– DELIGHTING IN
THE CHARACTER
OF GOD

15

'Great God of Wonders'

Whenever men think they have *fully* explained God it is a sure sign that they have misexplained him. It is, of course, right and proper that we should have and love our creeds and catechisms. It is both good and profitable for us to attempt to explain and define the doctrine of God for our own and others' benefit. But a wise Christian remembers that no formula or definition of God can comprehensively state *all* that is to be known of God. The creeds and the catechisms are good in that they give true definitions of God, but they do not pretend to be exhaustive. The finite cannot comprehend the infinite. If a formula could be devised for defining God comprehensively it would require to be as infinite as he is himself.

To think about God aright is the most exciting occupation possible for any created being. No doubt explorers who first tread on the soil of some uninhabited land feel awe and wonder at their privilege. Understandably, the scientist peering into his microscope at some hitherto unrecognized organism, or the astronomer who gazes at some far-flung galaxy, is breathless with rapture at the sight of what is so unknown and rare to man. But what are lost continents, or stars, or micro-organisms compared to the blessed and the living God?

The instrument by which man 'looks' at God is the mind. Our mind is the precious 'telescope' created within each man by our Maker himself to enable us to peer out beyond all created things and to 'see' God. To think right thoughts of God is the sum of all blessedness. Whether we call it theology, meditation, devotion or piety, the practice of fixing our thoughts on God till our hearts are 'strangely warmed' is the best bliss we can ever experience on this side of eternity. The mind is an in-built television by which a man may conjure up pictures which none sees but the man himself, and God. Thoughts spring up in our mind by thousands and ten thousands every hour of our waking existence. A man may train his thoughts. He may, and should, select some and shut out others. But one thought is instinctive to man – the realization that *God is*. The reason why the man who says there is no God is called 'a fool' (*Psa.* 14:1) is because he says what is untrue and what even he himself knows full well to be untrue.

No man really believes that there is no God. His mind informs him of God's existence. His heart may be hard, his background primitive, his knowledge of the Bible nothing at all. But yet his God-given intelligence tells him that he lives in the presence of the great Unseen Being. It is the misery of the godless man that he cannot get away from God; and the unspeakable comfort of the godly that he cannot be removed from God's presence.

Since all men know intuitively that God exists it is only by an act of perverse will-power that the wicked manage to shut God out even for a moment. It is called 'holding down the truth in unrighteousness' (*Rom.* 1:18). The sinner's instinct informs him that God is there and God is watching. But the sinner does not like God to be there and he has no wish for God to watch him. Hence the sinner must devise means whereby God is shut out from his mind. This whole world is a veritable store-house of devices invented by men over successive generations for shutting God out from the mind. It is done, or *may* be done, by means of music, or mirth, or alcohol, or a thousand things. The sinfulness of sin is seen in the myriad ways in which a sinner may use God's creation to exclude him from the mind as far as possible.

The fact that all sinners know instinctively that God exists goes far to explaining why the world is the place it is. Given the basic biblical truth that the sinner wishes to hide from God and to flee from him, it is to be expected that this world is going to be a labyrinth of dark tunnels of one sort or another for escaping from God, the great 'Enemy', as sinners so wrongly perceive him.

The sinner's life-long sad labour is to dig himself deep down into some place far away from his unloved and unwanted Maker. His own mind tells him that it cannot be done. But his furtive escape-act still goes on in spite of the illogicality of it. A sinner's life is therefore a fundamentally irrational thing. It is no better than that of a mouse in its treadmill. The mouse may run furiously and the wheel turn rapidly, but it is in the same place as before. Man can no more escape from God than from his own shadow. To run away from God's presence is impossible. The sinner's whole life is one life-long lie – alas, alas!

The only way to flee from the God of wrath is to flee to the God of mercy. The rational, as well as the religious, solution to the sinner's problem lies in running to God for his friendship and love. This, by God's unspeakable grace, is what every Christian learnt at his conversion. No small part of the 'peace' which we experience when we come back to God is in that we now no longer need to run along the labyrinthine ways of sin to try to avoid God. Our minds no longer need to live a lie. To come back to God is the single solution to every one of a sinner's problems. Other, lesser problems may remain but they are of small importance and of short duration.

It is a very great pity that Christian men do not use their minds more to think about the blessed being of God. If they would do so they would find it both an enriching and an exciting experience. It would renew the mind, refresh the soul and ennoble the life. If we meditated on God for half an hour each day we should all be better men. For God is the supreme and the ultimate object of thought and to think aright about God is to be transformed, if we have Christ as our Saviour, into the same image.

Every thought of God ends in mystery and produces wonder in our mind. It is instinctive to us to be amazed to think that God has no beginning, was not 'made', depends on nothing, but is eternally self-sufficient. It amazes us to recall that God is all around us yet remains invisible to us, that he is infinitely above us, yet infinitely present with us. It is awesome to consider that all creatures are the work of his hands, that all living things 'live and move and have their being' in him. It is breath-taking to grasp the thought that all events infallibly come to pass by God's secret decree and will, that the history of the world is slowly yet surely going to arrive at exactly the point which God eternally foreordained, and that all the powers of evil have, by their utmost rebelliousness, only fulfilled the role for which they were appointed. In a word, it is staggering to realize that we have such a God that 'of him, and through him, and to him are all things' and that his is the 'glory forever' (*Rom.* 11:36).

Whoever heard of the Holy Trinity who was not surprised at the thought of it? That God should be 'one' we can well understand. But the God who is 'one' is also 'three'. Our poor minds feel at once that we are in the presence of a Being who belongs to another and vastly higher order of things. By faith we receive the staggering revelation of a God who is three in Persons, yet one in essence. We believe and adore. But we are spellbound at the magnitude of the mystery. Our reaction is, with the angels and the great patriarchs of old, to fall down and to cover our faces.

And how deep are God's thoughts and ways! Our familiarity with Bible facts must not dull our sense of wonder. The fact is that we are spectators in this great universe. We behold the greatness and perceive something of the wisdom of God in all things. But we cannot pretend to know *why* God has acted as he has in all things – or, rather, we know only that everything is good and will glorify him at last. The rest we scarcely understand at all: Why a six-day creation? Why did God choose the Jews? Why so long before Christ came? Why so long before the Jews are brought into the church again? Why does sin seem to prevail so much and Satan to wield so much power? In all such musings we can only say to God, 'Even so, Father, for so it seemed good in thy sight' (*Matt.* 11:26).

Well do the holy Scriptures state, 'It is the glory of God to conceal a thing' (*Prov.* 25:2)! Could any man live if he saw into the future troubles of his life? We cannot, and need not, experience our miseries till they come upon us. God leads us along like blinkered horses so that we do not shy at the things we would otherwise see. Only Christ, of all mankind, saw and knew the full extent of his coming sufferings. He saw the Cross no doubt from his childhood and had a rehearsal of Gethsemane and Calvary every time he read his Old Testament. But he, being the God-Man, could bear it. We cannot!

How wise and true God is! Yet who believes him? The Scriptures, we say, are God's revelation. But who takes them seriously? Did the Jews, who read them so assiduously, understand that their nation would reject its own Messiah? Did Judas Iscariot see his own face in those portions of Scripture which had foretold his crime (*Psa.* 41:9; 55:12-14; 109:5f; *Zech.* 11:13) and which he had read, and even sung, a hundred times? Did the disciples of Christ believe in the Cross or the resurrection before these events happened? Do apostate churches today see themselves as those who, according to the apostolic writings, would one day commit apostasy? Have the popes seen themselves in Scripture? History not only teaches that history teaches nothing, but that even the Bible teaches most men nothing.

Man is blind to the light of God's Word because man is too sure that he understands what God means, whereas in fact man has often not understood at all.

We only start to understand God when we abase our proud minds before the majesty of his Word and cry out to him for light and grace. The correct attitude of mind is to treat God and all that belongs to him with proper reverence, love and fear. The wisdom of this world is foolishness with God and we only begin to be wise when we begin to think of him as 'the *only wise* God'. We do not need to be clever to be wise. What we do need is to have a humble heart and a contrite spirit.

God reserves his best blessings for those who truly love him. To them he gives not just blessings but himself. He has made all the elect restless and they have already a foretaste of perfect joy in Christ.

God has yet many wonders and great works to perform in this world. Some of them we shall not live to see. But already we see by faith the things which are to happen when the last page of history is finally turned: An end of all evil for God's people and everlasting joy upon their heads.

Our present duty is very clear. We are to live and work by faith. The 'great God of wonders' can be depended on to do all that the Bible says that he will do. Our part is simple enough. We are to seek to love him with all our heart and to rejoice in all his great goodness. What kind of meeting is that to be when God and his people at last come face to face and he rewards them according to the riches of his grace and glory!

16

God of Righteousness

All men become like the objects of their worship. Our inward character is being silently moulded by our view of God and our conception of him. Christian character is the fruit of Christian worship; pagan character the fruit of pagan religion; semi-Christian character the fruit of a half-true understanding of God. The principle holds good for us all: we become like what we worship – for worse or for better. 'They that make them are like unto them' (*Psa.* 115:8).

Since this is so, it follows that we must labour above all else to attain to as perfect a view of the character and being of God as we can. To go wrong in our idea of God is to go wrong everywhere else in our religion. This is probably the most difficult problem of all. It is the problem of problems. If only we knew God as he *is* and if only we thought of him and conceived of him as he *is*! If we came to that point, we should find ourselves standing on the highest pinnacle of all knowledge and we should then begin to make spiritual progress indeed. No wonder even Moses cried out to God: 'Show me thy glory'! (*Exod.* 33:18). We are not fit to lead others or to teach them till we have first seen the glory of God and come to appreciate his excellency and his supremacy.

The great game which Satan has played with mankind all throughout history has been to misrepresent God to us. Satan's trade is to put about false and counterfeit ideas of God. He did so in the beginning with catastrophic success: 'Yea, hath God said?' (*Gen.* 3:1). The energies of hell are being continually spent on this one project above all others: to portray God in false colours and in a false light. This is the devil's industry – to put a 'spin' on the true view of God. The history of religion is one long, sad commentary on the devil's propaganda-war against God. Let God be Zeus, or Jupiter, or Baal, or Thor, or anything at all. But let not God be God. Let God be wood, or stone, or gold, or bread, or 'the ground of being', or 'the great, universal spirit' or whatever you will. But let not God be what he is. No one has used the spin-doctor's art more successfully than the arch-enemy of our souls. His craft has been behind all idolatry, both ancient and modern. And modern idolatry is scarcely less damnable than that of the ancients.

Before any man can preach he must be brought to see God clearly for what he is. This is the first and greatest qualification of a prophet. He must know God in his essential character. The prophet is one who declares God to be what he is. Over against the hundred-and-one false views of God which prevail in this world, the prophet affirms God as God in truth. The genuine prophet is in this respect radically different from the false prophet. The false prophet conforms his view of God to that of popular opinion. His view of God does not offend anyone because the presentation which he makes of God is conventional and acceptable. The false prophet always presents a god who is tame and quiet. His god fits comfortably into the existing scheme of things. His god excites no wholesome fears, stirs no unwelcome qualms in the mind, disturbs no sleeping consciences, arouses no holy indignation, inspires no righteous revolution.

If the people want a golden calf, the weak prophet gives in to them. If the king and queen of the day patronize Baal-worship, the false prophets are ardent in their support. If the Roman emperor of the day claims to himself divine honours, the false prophet will oblige by offering on the altar his pinch of incense along with the others. He is a popular fellow.

The true prophet, however, is always unwelcome and unwanted. He is invariably so rude as to break through all the codes and conventions of his day. He points upwards to the God who is, and who is so different from what men want to hear concerning God. He points to a God who is righteous. He announces the God who is, above everything else, jealous of his own glory. He proclaims a God who is both law-giver and judge, a being who is transcendent and cannot be domesticated like a mere lap-dog whom sinners can stroke and need not fear.

This difference between true and false prophets is very noticeable all throughout Scripture. It explains why Moses, at the sight of the golden calf, threw down the tables of stone in holy indignation. It accounts for the behaviour of Micaiah the son of Imlah, who could not speak good of wicked king Ahab but only evil (*1 Kings* 22:8). It explains why Amos had the reputation for being a man who 'conspired' against the king (*Amos* 7:10). It gives the explanation for the untimely death of John the Baptist, of Stephen and of a host of other martyrs. They all proclaimed a righteous sin-hating God. Had they preached 'smooth things' (*Isa.* 30:10) they might have prolonged their lives.

The false gods are always 'intra-mundane'. That is to say, they belong to this world and are a part of this world. They are enclosed in the existing scheme of this world's affairs, and they smile benignly on mankind. The uncomfortable thing about the God of the Bible is that he insists on proclaiming himself to be above everything and everyone. He is 'God of gods' and 'Lord of lords'. There is no appeal from his sentence. Neither men nor governments can veto his decisions nor reverse his plans.

The true God is 'extra-mundane'. He is outside this little world in which we live, and he speaks of it in a way that makes us feel small. He sits on 'the circle of the earth, and the inhabitants thereof are as grasshoppers' (*Isa* 40:22). The God of the Bible plainly has no very great opinion of what we are apt to call 'human greatness'. He announces bluntly: 'Surely men of low degree are vanity, and men of high degree are a lie: to be laid in the balances, they are altogether lighter than vanity' (*Psa.* 62:9). This is a lesson which proud men have had to learn painfully. Pharoah had to learn it in his day. So did the Herods and the Caesars. So will every proud man in the end.

There is no one single question which our age and generation needs to face more than this: 'Who and what is God?' At the root of all the false religion and false worship in the world today is just this: ignorance of the character of God. The unholy haste with which men and churches are rushing to barter Bible truth for tradition or novelty is inspired by this very thing: ignorance of God. All the suave talk so often heard about 'unity and love', when it is not defined in biblical terms, is all a by-product of the same failure to study and understand the character of God.

It is a harder thing than many think to arrive at a true view of God's character and to hold on to it unswervingly. A true view of God must revolve around these two statements: 'God is light' (*1 John* 1:5) and 'God is love' (*1 John* 4:16). God is perfect in love and in holiness. Both are true. We are safe so long as we hold both in our minds together. We go astray as soon as we let go either. The church of the Middle Ages lost sight of a God of love; our age is in grave danger of losing sight of the holiness of this God of love.

When Christianity loses touch with righteousness it sinks down into baptized paganism. If the gospel of the love of God in Christ does not lift us up to love God's law and God's righteousness, it has not entered into our heart savingly. 'He that doeth righteousness is righteous even as he is righteous' (*1 John* 3:7). 'Whosoever doeth not righteousness is not of God, neither he that loveth not his brother' (*1 John* 3:10). Those who are here described as 'not of God' are certainly not just the irreligious outside the church but also, and more particularly, the religious within it who have had no saving change of heart.

Nominal Christians look for all the world like real Christians, except that they have neither love of the brethren nor love of righteousness. Love and righteousness are what spring up in the soul as soon as we are born of God. If they do not spring up in the soul, it is because the soul is still unchanged. Men are yet in their sins.

Whenever a race of men becomes obsessed with a sense of the love and righteousness of God, the world is turned upside down. It was so in the time of Christ and his apostles. It was so at the Protestant Reformation. The hearts of Luther, Calvin and Knox were aflame with love of truth and righteousness. They were men whom God mastered. They had the true view of his character as the God of perfect love and light, not love only but light and righteousness also. They saw their calling to be to plead for truth and to do justice at all costs. They could never have braved the opposition unless they had first come to know God in a most powerful way as the God who is 'over all' and 'blessed forever' (*Rom.* 9:5).

The manner in which men know God is reflected in the degree to which they appreciate his claims on their lives. Recent times, sadly, have produced a great deal of wayward Christian worship and practice, and this is the proof that our knowledge of God has been only small. We have heard of the zeal for righteousness of Cromwell, Whitefield and Chalmers. But the thing that marked them as great Christians has been seen of late in all too few, in spite of all our modern privileges.

The power of true religion is in its passion to apply the principles of righteousness to all the practical affairs of our life on earth: at home, at work, in church, in society and in national life. The apostles state this in their epistles over and over again. Our difficulty today is this: Where shall we begin in our modern societies, where righteousness is almost dead and buried? We might begin by acquainting ourselves better with the God of righteousness himself, and then beseech him to stretch out his mighty arm again.

17

The 'Slowness' of God's Ways

God is pleased to work his purposes out often, if not always, in a sort of 'slow motion'. If God's people had it within their own power to execute the eternal plans they would do everything far more quickly. The urge in our souls is to have things done at a great rate. Though piety forbids the prayer coming to our lips, the thought is often in the hearts of God's children, 'Why is God so slow in his ways?' The churches of Christ make their progress through time ever so slowly and our sanctification itself goes forward at a painfully slow pace. On the other hand, the powers of darkness have generous scope given to them to impede every good effort which Christians put forth to glorify God. The whole world in which we live, like our own gardens, is prolific in weeds of every sort but very sparing of the fruits and flowers of righteousness. The one grow up overnight; the other only after months and years of toil and disappointment.

The above reflection becomes more painful, not less so, as we become more familiar with the sovereign character of God. The problem which we feel over God's seeming 'slowness' when we have low views of his greatness is not so pressing as it becomes when we see him more clearly. If God in some sense 'needs' us to 'help him' against the forces of evil, we are not greatly puzzled that these dark forces are so successful in resisting the gospel. Their success, we might suppose, is owing to *our* human failure to give God the 'needed' assistance in doing his great work. God is 'doing his part', we might imagine, 'but *we* are letting him down and it is no wonder that we see Satan so successful'.

There is an element of truth in this view of our service to God. Unfaithfulness on our part may well be rewarded with failure. But it would be a shallow view of God to suppose that he could fail for want of 'help' from us. Omnipotence, by definition, can do all it wishes without help from any. Even the little we give of strength and ability to God is his own gift. We never 'help' God in the sense of adding anything to his powers or resources. 'Of him, and through him, and to him are all things' (*Rom.* 11:36).

It is this very fact which makes it so painful to observe the seeming 'slowness' of God's work in the world. The gospel conquered the Roman Empire in three centuries. But then it fell into decline for a thousand years. The vast mission-fields of the world had to wait long centuries before a Carey, a Martyn and a Livingstone ventured to take the light to them. The Jews have been in darkness for almost two millennia and still show small evidence of their future re-grafting into the church of Christ (*Rom.* 11:23). How many tribes on earth are still to this day without a Bible! How many Middle Eastern countries are closed to gospel work! How much decline we see in the West! How much apostasy in the visible church! If Christians were to walk by sight and not by faith the church would have been eaten up with despair and paralysed with inertia many centuries ago.

We must suppose that the 'slowness' of God's ways, as we perceive it, is itself a wonderful part of the eternal plan. It is the fruit of God's perfect wisdom. In this, as in all other respects, 'the foolishness of God is wiser than men' and 'the weakness of God is stronger than men' (*1 Cor.* 1:25). If we are to act wisely in the service of God we must learn to *attempt* much, but be patient in our expectations and to labour on against set-backs, obstacles, problems, opposi-tions and disappointments. We must defy that indefinable agony of soul which comes on the Christian when he sees that Satan has been permitted to blast his best efforts for a time.

If the Christian worker adopts the attitude and outlook of the businessman and estimates spiritual work only in outward terms of visible progress and success, he will almost certainly fall into the snare of having to compro-mise the standards and principles of God's Word. Spiritual progress is something which man cannot measure. The farmer sows his seed and hopes, confidently perhaps, for a crop in the autumn. But the preacher or missionary may have to wait long years before he sees the harvest-time. The preacher, or the missionary, like the farmer, sows in hope but the season of reaping is hidden from him. In the meantime he must go on patiently sowing the good seed of God's Word into human hearts. He must 'hope against hope' (*Rom.* 4:18) through the long dreary times in which the Word of God seems not to bring forth any visible fruit in the lives of men.

However hard it is for flesh and blood to wait for God to 'give the increase' (*1 Cor.* 3:7) – ten years perhaps, or twenty, or more still – the Christian who labours for God must look constantly to his hidden hope. This hope is the sure promise of God that 'in due season we shall reap if we faint not' (*Gal.* 6:9). All gospel-work is to be carried out in faith and in hope. We do not yet see what the results will be. Our hope of gospel success, like the greater hope of heaven, is a hope which is 'not seen' (*Rom.* 8:24). We must 'with patience wait for it' (*Rom.* 8:25).

It is at this very point that a powerful temptation assails every faithful Christian worker. It is the secret voice in his ear which whispers to him that he would be more successful if he abandoned God's methods and resorted to methods of his own. 'If God's message does not bring results, why not adjust the message to suit men's tastes?' 'If I am to get the numbers up I must surely be allowed to preach the gospel in imaginative ways.' 'The old gospel and mere preaching do not work any more and so we need to use a little of the world's methods.' It is all too easy to find justification for changing both our message and the worship of God if once we begin to listen to the whispered voice of temptation.

Just about every species of novelty and every form of unfaithfulness to Christ has been justified by one or other plausible pretext. 'We must be positive and not negative.' So the preacher never speaks of death, judgment or eternal punishment in hell. 'We must be contemporary.' So the pulpit omits large areas of truth which are vital to Christian sanctification and knowledge. 'We must make our hearers happy as they go home.' So we hear very little of repentance, mortification of sin or of taking up our cross and denying ourselves. 'We must attract the outsider at all costs.' So worship is 'modernized' till it differs little from entertainment. The whispered voice in the preacher's ear – or perhaps rather in the ears of some in his congregation – becomes the real source of authority for what is done at the services of worship in God's house.

If there is one text more than another which deserves to be printed on church calendars and text-cards in our times it is surely this: 'Behold, to obey is better than sacrifice, and to hearken than the fat of rams. For rebellion is as the sin of witchcraft, and stubbornness is as iniquity and idolatry' (*1 Sam.* 15:22–23). This is admittedly a very demanding text of Scripture. It obliges us first of all to become diligent students of God's Word till we are sure we know what he really requires us to preach and how he requires us to worship him. Then it tests our nerve to the uttermost because we may have to face the possibility that God may not always seem to 'bless' our obedient adherence to his Word in our preaching and our worship. At least, God's blessing may appear to us to be less than we want and revival to come more slowly than we expected. It is at this very point that temptation either to alter God's message or else to invent our own methods becomes acute.

King Saul's patience was exhausted when Samuel delayed beyond a certain day. He could bear the strain no longer and he took matters into his own hands by foolishly offering to God a burnt-offering irregularly. His own confession later to Samuel was: 'I *forced* myself' (*1 Sam.* 13:12). When, still more foolishly, he repeated the same sin later he had to admit: 'I have sinned . . . because I feared the people, and obeyed their voice' (*1 Sam.* 15:24). The temptation to disobey God always arises from pride and ambition on our part or else, as in Saul's case here, from fear of man.

If, in our service to Jesus Christ, we aim to be faithful we need to set our minds steadfastly to resist these influences of ambition and fear. The call of the hour is for servants of the Master who will be true to 'the whole counsel of God' in their preaching and resolve in their aim to behave properly in the house of God. To do otherwise may have the appearance of giving the preacher some advantage in terms of popularity or usefulness. But every departure he makes from the Word of God in order to purchase such an 'advantage' will appear in the end to have been achieved at too high a price. Not only will compromise take something away from our eternal reward; it will produce a harvest of trouble for Christ's people in time to come.

Why is God so 'slow' in working? Partly, no doubt, in order to try our obedience to his written Word. Why does God delay in sending revival? Partly, we may suppose, in order to give our knowledge and faith a wholesome trial, and to prove the purity and sincerity of our motives in serving him. It is poor service if we take occasion from it to alter what God has said in order to gain human applause or some other personal advantage. The 'slowness' of God's ways tries us all, searches out our real motives, and tests our real commitment to what he has commanded us to say and do.

If God sometimes appears to us to work 'too slowly' we must call to our attention the great fact that his Word never alters. The gospel, even the 'old-fashioned gospel', is never out of date. It is still the only message that will change man's heart and lift him to heaven. To preach the Word fully and faithfully is the greatest service we can ever render to God in this life. It is no proof that he is not blessing us that we may not at this hour be seeing great revivals or witnessing great numbers of conversions. There are days in the history of the Church when we have to preach the Word not only 'in season' but also '*out of season*' (*2 Tim.* 4:2). Christ will not blame us for preaching faithfully in a dark day in which there are few conversions. But he will blame us if we mix error with his gospel on the pretext that it will be more successful.

Similarly, it will be to our shame and discredit if we alter the worship of God by introducing our own inventions to please the carnal minds of men. What, after all, is 'worship', but an offering to God of what he himself has required? Everything else is 'will-worship' (*Col.* 2:23) and God says of it, 'In vain do they worship me, teaching for doctrines the commandments of men' (*Matt.* 15:9). Worship is not doing something to draw people to church, though it often has that effect. It is first and foremost the offering of praise to God because he is worthy to receive it, and because he requires it.

'But will God never visit us again to do a speedy and great work of revival?' Undoubtedly he will, and we must bend every nerve to pray and plead for his gracious visitation. While he tarries, however, we must make no golden calf.

18

God's Secrets – the Believer's Comforts

God's wisdom is seen in the way in which he both reveals himself and also conceals himself. A perfect economy is exercised by God in the degree of his self-revelation and self-concealment. Just enough of God is revealed to leave us 'without excuse' (*Rom.* 1:20) if we choose to ignore him; and enough is revealed for those who believe in him to be fully assured of him. By this arrangement, God's wisdom has left room for doubt in all who prefer to doubt him, and room enough for sure confidence in all who trust him.

God is glorified in this manner, because in this way he places all mankind under a life-long test as to whether we shall trust him or not. The nature of all God's dealings therefore in this life is to place us always in a situation in which we are required to take him on trust. We are on trial in this life in all that we do. Every decision we make is a test of our moral character and indicates, more or less, what we think about God. The friendships we make, the places we go to, the plans we form are all more or less an index of our attitude towards God. Even our inward doubts and fears about situations in life reflect the way we either believe and trust God, or else doubt and distrust him.

God has constructed man's life on earth in this way not accidentally but purposely, because in this life, all through life, we are on probation. The final Judgment Day will be the assessment of how we have lived and it will announce to all the world both what we have thought of God and what, as a consequence, we deserve to enjoy, or else suffer, in eternity.

The way in which God has chosen most especially to reveal himself is by a spoken and written revelation of his will for our life. Whilst it is perfectly true that something of God is seen and known in the created universe, not enough is known by that means to tell us how to live. The created world is full of evidences of the existence of a great and good Creator. But of itself the created world does not explain how, in detail, I am to live my daily life.

The glorious sun and sky, the beautiful earth and the expansive sea excite the mind to admiration and delight; but they do not inform me as to how I should live and behave, worship and pray, think and speak. The universe was intended by God to be a *general* revelation of himself – a startlingly wonderful evidence of his Unseen Being. But the universe does not tell me where I may find this great God that I may love and enjoy him forever. In addition to this general revelation a *special,* verbal revelation was needed.

The first verbal and special revelation of himself which God gave to man, was in the form of a command, giving him permission to eat of all the trees in paradise except one. The penalty for eating of *this* tree would be death (*Gen.* 2:16,

17). Having given to man this revelation of his will, God withdrew and concealed himself. Not only so, but more importantly still, he exposed man to temptation to test his obedience to what had now been said.

The form of man's first temptation is full of instruction for us still because temptation always takes this form. Man had a sure word from God. The question was: would he, in the absence of God and under the pressure of Satan's evil suggestion, keep to what God had commanded, or not? It was of course possible for God to have protected man from this temptation or to have greatly reduced the force of the temptation by revealing himself to Adam while Satan presented the temptation. But it was God's will to leave man to face the pressure of Satan's suggestion without the comfortable, felt presence of God. The intention on God's part is plain to see. He conceals himself to test man's obedience to the word which has been spoken: 'Thou shalt *not* eat' (*Gen.* 2:17).

This first temptation is the pattern, or paradigm, of all temptations which we ever face. The main elements are all here: a word from God, pressure from an alien influence to disobey, and a profound moral choice to be faced up to by man. God conceals himself for a time to observe how we shall act in such a situation.

A moment's reflection will assure us that this statement is true and accurate. The temptations of all whom we read of in the Bible are the same in form and character. Lot's wife had a word from God: 'Escape for thy life; look not behind thee' (*Gen.* 19:17). But under the weight of her own carnal affections she disobeyed and looked back and so became a pillar of salt. David knew the seventh commandment, but under the power of his own lust, he swept aside all restraint and both sinned and suffered afterwards. So, too, Christ felt the temptation to turn the stones into bread in his hour of hunger. But a perfect obedience to God's revealed will gave him a perfect restraint.

In all temptations the issue is the same: 'Shall I go by the word of a God whom I cannot see or by the word of some other being?' The acutely sharp focus in temptation is on this one thing: 'What do I think of God? Is what he has said true? Is there some way round what he has said or must I take him at his word when he is invisible and 'far away'?

The history of Old Testament Israel and of the New Testament Church is one long, detailed and extended commentary on the first temptation of mankind. In proportion as Israel and its leaders lived by faith in the invisible God whose Book they had in their hands, they were blessed and made progress. In proportion as they allowed other influences to shape their life and conduct, they declined and fell back. Those who are commended in God's Word are said to have 'endured as seeing him who is invisible' (*Heb.* 11:27). Others are held up as a warning in that they 'forgot God' (*Psa.* 106:21). The same is true of the New Testament churches and of ourselves to this day.

It is amazing, considering how much light we have on the evil of forgetting God and his Word, how hard we find it to remember God and to live by faith! The theory can be stated in a few words. But the practice we find intensely difficult. Even when we profess to believe in an infallible Bible, we are far from an infallible practice!

That this is so is a reminder to us of how little we really believe in God or in the Bible. If we fully believed that the unseen eye of a holy God is always upon us, we should care nothing for the praise of men or for their frowns. Perfect faith says that it must obey God even if it has to displease near friends and family. 'He that loveth father or mother more than me is not worthy of me; and he that loveth son or daughter more than me is not worthy of me' (*Matt.* 10:37).

It is for this reason that Christ stated: 'Think not that I am come to send peace on earth; I came not to send peace, but a sword' (*Matt.* 10:34). The unbelieving world can tolerate those who will go *so far* in their practice of religion. But it hates those who put God and his words before *all* considerations of happiness in this world. The believer does just this because he lives 'as seeing him who is invisible' (*Heb.* 11:27). In this spirit, the young child Jesus said to his mother, 'Wist ye not that I must be about my Father's business?' (*Luke* 2:49). To upset a loved parent is permissible for duty's sake; to offend God is never permissible for any reason.

The claims of God are remote to one who thinks of him as little better than a polite fiction. But these same claims are imperative in the conscience of one who remembers who and what God is. It is this factor which explains the paradox of Christ: 'He that findeth his life shall lose it: and he that loseth his life for my sake, shall find it' (*Matt.* 10:39). Put Christ first, and the world's easy style of life vanishes at once. The wholehearted Christian becomes dead to many of the common comforts of this life. But he will find heaven at last and all its superior comforts will be his forever. Put yourself first and you may have the name of 'Christian', but you will lose your soul. It is the universal rule always.

If all this is so, how can any Christian be happy in this life? If a believer experiences 'the loss of all things' (*Phil.* 3:8) here below, what is the explanation for his present comfort and joy? The answer is in the words: 'The secret of the LORD is with them that fear him' (*Psa.* 25:14). Just as God himself is hidden from our eye in this life, so are his inward comforts hidden from the eye of all who are not his people. The believer has from God in this life more joy in his heart than the unbeliever has from all his outward pleasures (*Psa.* 4:7).

Hidden from the eye and ear of unbelievers but revealed to the soul of those who love him, God's comforts are his secrets to his children. So the apostle puts the matter: 'Eye hath not seen, nor ear heard, neither have entered into the heart of man, the things which God hath prepared for them that love him. But God hath revealed them unto us by his Spirit: for the Spirit searcheth all things, yea, the deep things of God' (*1 Cor.* 2:9–10). All the doctrines of Scripture bring joy and comfort to a believer in one way or another. The words of the unseen God are a wellspring of joy, a treasury of hope, an encyclopedia of encouragement to him to persevere in the life of faith so that he may 'inherit all things' (*Rev.* 21:7).

Oh what secrets God has revealed to his children! He has shown them how a loving Saviour became 'bone of our bone and flesh of our flesh' (*Eph.* 5:30) that he might wash us from guilt and make us his Bride in eternity to come. He has expounded to us the mystery of imputation that we might know how the Christ who 'became sin for us' is now 'the righteousness of God' to us (*2 Cor.* 5:21). He has told us of the coming glories of heaven and informed us that a place is even now being prepared for us there. He has revealed to us that though our body be burnt to ashes it will rise again at last in glory, honour and immortality.

In this world, God has been largely invisible to man. The rule of life in this present world is that we 'walk by faith, not by sight' (*2 Cor.*5:7). This is the way ordained in this lower world. But it will not be the way we shall live in the world to come, which Christ will introduce at last. There, in the rejuvenated universe, righteousness will be the character of all the redeemed. Not only so, but they shall 'see his face', and his 'name shall be in their foreheads' (*Rev.* 22:4).

This beatific vision of God in Christ is the prize which he has throughout the ages revealed in the hearts of all who have loved him. The Bible will not be out of date till that day. Meanwhile, let us strive to walk by it as our only rule 'till the day dawn and the day star arise in our hearts' (*2 Pet.* 1:19).

19

The Gentleness of Christ

There is scarcely anything more awesome than to watch almighty power at work. It is this that we see at creation.

The will of God is here seen at work exerting itself upon nothing and calling worlds into existence from non-existence. The sudden eruption of space, time, galaxies and intelligent beings into being out of nothing is a concept which, however familiar to the devout Bible reader, must never be allowed to lose its wonder and its fascination. From God all beings receive their existence and we, as intelligent beings, should try to live daily in the consciousness that the God whose all-powerful word called us into existence is 'over all' and 'blessed forever'. It is profane to take our Creator's work for granted.

But if almighty power is awesome to us, it is still more awesome to see absolute power acting with absolute gentleness. It is this that we see in the life and behaviour of the Lord Jesus Christ. He was sent into our world with all the power that is inherently his as the eternal Son of God. That is to say, he came to take our nature without in any way laying aside the powers that belonged eternally to his own divine nature and person. And we see in the life of Christ a perfect example of meekness, lowliness and gentleness. It is possible to talk sentimentally about the gentleness of Christ as though it were something obvious or commonplace. But in fact this gentleness of our Saviour is something which we should look upon as remarkable in the highest degree. A moment's thought will assure us that Christ's lowliness and tenderness is quite as amazing as the most dramatic of all his miracles. Let us examine it for a moment.

The history of our world is very much the history of how power has been abused by men and nations. Dictators and tyrants have risen up on the stage of this world and for a little time they have ruled over men with pitiless terror. Empires have sprung up which have absorbed weaker and poorer nations and often, if not quite always, ruled with oppression and exploitation. If mankind's tyrants have not been entirely successful in crushing our human race absolutely, it is not for want of the will to do it. One thing alone has prevented them from dominating the whole world – lack of power. If the Pharaohs and the Caesars, the Napoleons and the Hitlers of this world had only had sufficient power they would never have stopped till the whole human race was grovelling at their feet.

But the history of our world shows us one man who *did* have power to do whatever he willed. Jesus of Nazareth came into the world invested with infinite and unlimited power. He entered into history endowed with all the omnipotence of Godhood. This power he was pleased to display before the eyes of men on numerous occasions. We refer to these displays of his power as 'miracles'. The miracles were the exercise of Christ's infinitely powerful will on the material world of his day. So that men would not be in any doubt about the absolutely all-inclusive scope of his almightiness, Christ exerted it in a multitude of ways. He stilled the storm, banished sickness, restored sight, cast out Satan, cleansed leprosy, walked on the sea, raised the dead. The most consummately wonderful miracle of all was his own rising again from the dead. He *conquered* death and overcame it.

The one figure in all mankind's history who *did* have power to crush the world under his heel, had he but wished to do so, is the world's supreme example of meekness and gentleness. Never do we see Christ use his power harshly, cruelly or vindictively. Once and only once perhaps do we have a hint of how Jesus might have used his power against his enemies if he had chosen to do so. It was in the garden of Gethsemane when his betrayer and those with him approached the person of our Lord to lay hands on him. The Apostle John records the event: 'As soon then as he had said unto them, I am he, they went backward, and fell to the ground' (*John* 18:6).

On this one occasion, so far as we know, did the Lord Jesus put forth just so much of his divine power that his enemies fell backward on the ground. We can scarcely think that they fell backwards for any other reason. We are not informed that Jesus let out a supernaturally loud shout or that he menaced them in any way. Such conduct is entirely out of character with all that the Gospels tell us of Christ in any case. The true explanation must be that he exerted at that moment just a little of that omnipotent power which he had used in the creation of the world. It was not intended to do his attackers any harm but it ought to have been enough to tell them that in arresting Christ they were arresting Omnipotence itself.

It is possible to sentimentalize the gentleness of Christ in another way. We must never portray him as if he had any degree of moral weakness or as if he were tolerant of sin. Christ was 'a friend of publicans and sinners' (*Matt.* 11:19) in one sense. He 'received sinners and ate with them' (*Luke* 15:2). So much is true, but it must not be stated in such a way as to imply something false. Our Saviour's gentle treatment of the erring and the sinning sons of men is never to be portrayed as if he had an easy attitude towards their sins and errors.

Some preachers and writers do imply this. They give the impression of a Christ who is tolerant of sin. This is not true. He was patient and even tender with sinners but he never condoned their sin. His gentleness is seen in pardoning the penitent, not in excusing their past behaviour. 'Go and sin no more' (*John* 8:11) he says to one. 'Her sins which are many are forgiven' (*Luke* 7:47), he says of another. 'Sin no more lest a worse thing befall thee' (*John* 5:14), he says to a third. The gentleness of Christ is shown in his readiness to allow sinners to come close to him for his blessing, healing and pardon.

There are limits, too, to the gentleness of Christ in his dealings with sinners. If we overstate this aspect of his character and ministry we shall distort our picture of him. The evidence shows that on occasion our Lord was angry (*Mark* 3:5) with sinners. He spoke out bluntly and boldly on many occasions when he saw a carnal wisdom and hypocrisy in religious leaders. He made a whip of small cords and drove out those who were turning the house of God into a den of thieves. This he did both at the beginning and at the end of his ministry (*John* 2:15; *Mark* 11:15). Scarcely any more stern or denunciatory language can be found in all the Word of God than that which the Lord Jesus Christ uses in his exposure of the foolish and blind ways in which the Pharisees had corrupted the gospel of the grace of God in his day (*Matt.* 23).

The character of meekness which we see in the Saviour in the pages of the four Gospels is one which we ought to study and imitate as his disciples. There should never be anything 'loud' or flashy about a believer or about his religious behaviour. The religion of Jesus is one which breeds circumspection, depth of soul, self-restraint and genuineness. The believer, and especially the Christian minister, needs to walk in Christ's steps in this, as in all other respects. We are to be compassionate towards the lost sinners of this world. But we are never to make them feel at ease in their sins. The ideal we see in Christ is reflected in the lives of his servants. They are a blend of two excellencies: deep mercy and shining purity.

This quality of gentleness in Christ is an expression of the love which he bears to men's souls. He did not come to condemn the world but to save it (*John* 3:17). While this present world stands he will be most patient with sinners. 'A bruised reed shall he not break, and smoking flax shall he not quench, till he send forth judgment unto victory' (*Matt.* 12:20). He is supremely patient with his own people. He bears with our infirmities and pardons our life-long sinfulness.

The danger is that through presumption it is possible for men, and even for churches, to abuse the patience of Christ. Nothing provokes him to lay aside his gentleness so much as when we presume to disobey his Word on the pretext that he is too loving to be provoked. It is only the fool who confuses meekness with weakness, or who imagines that because Christ is slow to anger he will *never* be angry. Let us glory in the compassion of Christ; but woe betide us if we take advantage of it! Those who take advantage of Christ's kindness so as to indulge in worldliness, carnality and disobedience will discover that they have turned a Lamb into a Lion.

None are so terrible in anger as those who are slow to anger. So is Christ. He says as much to the seven churches in Asia (*Rev.* 2–3). He means to be taken seriously when he says: 'I will kill her children with death; and all the churches shall know that I am he which searcheth the reins and hearts: and I will give unto every one of you according to your works' (*Rev.* 2:23). Gentle as our Saviour is with the penitent, the lowly, the needy and the prayerful, he is nevertheless dreadful when men tamper with his truth, distort his gospel, pollute his church or live with secret sins.

What need we all have of a Saviour who is perfect in patience! What need we have of One who is full of grace! Such is the Son of God who died for us. Out of obedience and respect for him we do well to walk in the light of his Word and keep ourselves unspotted from the world.

20

No Greater Love

As Christians we can put up cheerfully with all manner of trials provided we feel a sense of Christ's love. This is the key to Christians' courage all through history. They have sung God's praises while they suffered the lash as galley-slaves. They have been beside themselves with ecstasy in prisons, in chains, in torments and in fire because they have felt the love of Christ poured upon their hearts. Like Stephen, they have scorned the pains of stoning because they have seen the Son of God before their minds. The blood of the martyrs is the seed of the church because Christ has been with them in the fires.

No experience is better for the soul than to feel the love of Christ. It was with this that Christ prepared his disciples as they faced life without his visible presence. He was concerned in the Upper Room (*John* 13–17) to assure and re-assure them of his love, a love which would not diminish after he was removed from their sight but which would bring them, and all like them, to the glory of heaven at last.

The Upper-Room discourse was Christ's tender farewell to those who would soon have to face the whole cruel world after his decease.

With a foresight of their coming trials and martyrdom, our Lord prepares the disciples for their undreamed-of labours and sufferings, successes and triumphs in his Name by expounding to them the evidences of his affection for them. 'Let not your heart be troubled: ye believe in God, believe also in me' (*John* 14:1). 'I go to prepare a place for you' . . . I will come again and receive you unto myself' (14:2–3). 'I am in the Father, and the Father in me' (14:1, 10). 'Whatsoever ye shall ask . . . I will do' (14:13). 'He shall give you another Comforter' (14:16). 'Peace I leave with you' (14:27). 'These things have I spoken unto you, that my joy might remain in you, and that your joy might be full' (15:11). 'Love one another as I have loved you. Greater love hath no man than this, that a man lay down his life for his friends. Ye are my friends' (15:12–14). With these and many other similar words of sweetness our Lord strengthened the hearts of those whom he loved in this world. And he still strengthens those who are his to this day.

We must not fail to notice that this entire section of our Lord's ministry (*John* 13–17) begins and ends with reference to his love for those who are his true disciples. The passage begins and ends with Christ's love, 'Having loved his own which were in the world, he loved them unto the end' (13:1). So the Upper-Room discourse begins. So too it closes as our Lord concludes his great prayer: 'That the love wherewith thou hast loved me may be in them, and I in them' (17:26). It is clear that this latter reference to Christ's love refers to what all his people are to experience eternally at last. The church's destiny is defined by the terms here of this High-Priestly prayer. It is to be a destiny in which we shall know, with all the saints, eternal unity of soul, suffused with glory and love (17:21, 22, 24, 26). In heaven the cream and top of all our delights will be to enjoy the sense of God's love for us in Christ forever.

Some of the joys of heaven are postponed till we arrive there. The beatific vision of the ever-blessed Triune God cannot be seen by any in this life and will not be seen till we get to glory. And so it is with many other blessings of heaven. But not so with the love of Christ. This can be known by believers here and now, and it *is* known by them.

The Christian who claims to *feel* Christ's love for him is no fanatic but a genuine New Testament believer. It is true, Christ's love in the soul is a mystery which we cannot fully explain. But it is a reality which we would be wrong to suppress or deny. The Acts of the Apostles is an incomprehensible book unless we see that the early Christians were daily feasting on Christ, daily aware in experience of his love, and daily seeking to please him in this life. How else can we explain their holy boldness, their contempt for outward sufferings, their disdain for spurious ecclesiastical authority? For them all, as for Paul, the saying was true: 'For me to live is Christ' (*Phil.* 1:21).

The Apostle Paul could hardly forgive himself for his cruel persecution of the Lord's people in his unregenerate days. But, for all his awareness of past sin and ignorance, he does not hide the experience which followed him everywhere, of feeding on Christ's felt love for him. 'The love of Christ constraineth us' (*2 Cor.* 5:14). 'The love of God is shed abroad in our hearts' (*Rom.* 5:5). 'God commendeth his love toward us' (*Rom.* 5:8). 'Who shall separate us from the love of Christ?' (*Rom.* 8:35). 'His great love wherewith he loved us' (*Eph.* 2:4). 'Rooted and grounded in love' (*Eph.* 3:17). 'To know the love of Christ which passeth knowledge' (*Eph.* 3:19). Our sins, however dark they have been, must not become to us a cloud that obscures the light of Christ's loving face for us as his people.

The love of Jesus Christ is not in word or promise only. It does not consist of fair speeches only, or sweet utterances of the mouth. Christ has demonstrated his love for us as his people by his mighty redemptive actions. 'He loved me and gave himself for me' (*Gal.* 2:20). That is why the Christian can never stop talking about the Cross and the blood of his Saviour. To the hypocrite these are offensive things. The false Christian would much prefer to think of Christ's love apart from the Cross, and the blood that was shed there on it. But the true child of God glories in the Cross as the supreme evidence of his Saviour's love. The blood and sweat of Gethsemane, the agony and darkness of Calvary are to the real Christian the tangible expressions of his glorious Redeemer's love for him.

He who would make any progress in his knowledge of Christ's love must meditate often on the blood-shedding and sorrow of Jesus. 'The Son of God loved me', let every Christian say, 'before I had any existence or any being. While he was making the universe his love was set on me. I was in his thoughts in eternity past. Even when as yet there was no world, no paradise, no sin, I was in his mind. He looked along the corridors of time and his intention was, even at that time, to come for me and to rescue me. All through history he saw me and his zeal stirred him to come into this dark world to take me home to glory.'

As a woman with no children goes to an orphanage and takes from it a child for herself, so Christ came into this orphanage of a world to remove us from it and take us home. As a wealthy man might see his heart's desire in a poor beggar-woman and make of her his bride, so Christ looked on his poor people and in his love and pity he lifted them from the dunghill to become his spouse and bride, 'members of his body, of his flesh and of his bones' (*Eph.* 5:30; see also Genesis 2:23).

It is not difficult for the true believer to hate his sins or to confess them to God. He hates them because they are what occasioned the damnation of the One whom now he loves. It is not hidden from a true believer's eye that if Christ is our righteousness, then we were his condemnation, and our sins the occasion of his death.

It is a strange relationship that the believer has with his own sin. He does it against his deepest desire and he is hearty in deploring the evil of his shortcomings. If he could only lay aside his sin he would do so at once and for ever. He hates what he does amiss because sin is the very contradiction of God. The Christian who sins easily is either an ignorant Christian or no Christian at all.

Backsliding in the soul always begins with a decline in our love for the Saviour himself. We grow cold towards the

One who died for us. It is possible for the Christian to be active long after he has declined in his love to Jesus. A man may go on with his preaching, or writing, or serving, long after his heart has ceased to feel the warmth of its first love to the Lord whom he still attempts to serve.

But all our service is second-rate if it does not come from a heart of burning love to our Master. No words are more terrible than those heard by the church at Ephesus: 'Thou hast left thy first love' (*Rev.* 2:4). They were very orthodox and very busy in Christian work; but they had lost the lustre of their first love. Christ has little love for cold-hearted service.

Perhaps our greatest need as Christians is to rise above the habitual coolness with which we treat the love of Christ. If Jesus Christ is God and died for me, as a great missionary once said, then no sacrifice is too great for me to make for him. Let every believer say the same. Let every believer remind himself that we deserve, one and all, to be cast away forever into the outer darkness. It is mercy that we have been spared this judgment which we richly deserved. Have I forgotten that I am what I am because Christ laid down his life?

Whatever of philanthropy or public-spiritedness we shall ever read of in this history of our poor human race, we shall not meet with any who did for us what Jesus Christ has done. Where do we find any, apart from our Lord Jesus Christ, who drank lovingly the cup of our damnation? Kings and great men have, for the most part, spent their energies on conquering empires and amassing wealth for themselves. But Jesus Christ, and he alone, chose the way of poverty and gave his soul to be an offering for our sins. It was

Christ's one great passion to glorify God by raising us all up to the glory of heaven.

The secret of Christianity is that it makes men ready and willing to 'count all things but dung' for Christ's sake (*Phil.* 3:8). It makes men willing to be despised and even counted 'as the filth of the world, and the offscouring of all things' (*1 Cor.* 4:13) for the love they bear to Christ. But no man will venture all for Christ till he has *tasted* richly of his love within his soul. Such love is described as a being 'filled with all the fulness of God' (*Eph.* 3:19). It is, in other words, the best experience possible in earth or heaven. It is a 'knowing' of 'the love of Christ which passeth knowledge' (*Eph.* 3:19). To know this in the heart here and now is to have a heaven before heaven. No wonder Christ himself said, 'Greater love hath no man than this' (*John* 15:13).

THE LIFE OF GRACE
– UNDERSTANDING
GOD'S TRUTH

21

'I Am the Truth'

When Pontius Pilate asked 'What is truth?', he betrayed the deep cynicism which lies at the heart of all irreligious men. He revealed the sad fact that when men do not believe in God, it is not that they believe in nothing but that they believe in anything. To the irreligious mind there is no such thing as truth. The irreligious man is all his lifetime drifting in a sea of uncertainty without chart or compass. He knows neither where he came from nor where he is going. He is 'blown about by every wind of doctrine' (*Eph.* 4:14). He is compared to 'wandering stars' (*Jude* 13) which appear somewhere in the universe for a time and then vanish into the outer darkness. To the irreligious mind there is no ultimate meaning to life. It is a 'tale told by an idiot, full of sound and fury, signifying nothing'.

From this tragic meaninglessness every Christian is saved and delivered by the gracious power of Jesus Christ. To be a Christian is to be a believer in truth, in reality, and in the meaningfulness and purpose of life. The newly converted person rejoices to be able now to see his life, not as adrift in a dark ocean, but lived within the framework of a wise and intelligent purpose. He has the unspeakably comforting experience of looking up and recognizing that he belongs to the great God and lives his life within the framework of a fixed divine plan which is all-embracing and which takes care of every detail of life. It even takes care of the things beyond life in this present world and makes a full provision for a happy eternity to come.

The Lord Jesus Christ clearly had a passion for truth. He declared that his very life's mission was to 'bear witness unto the *truth*' (*John* 18:37). In an oft-quoted text, he even went so far as to affirm, 'I am the *truth*' (*John* 14:6). Christ is 'the *true* light' (*John* 1:9). His high-priestly prayer shows that his concern for all his people is that they 'might be sanctified through the *truth*'. He even defines his believing people in the same terms: 'Every one that is of the *truth* heareth my voice' (*John* 18:37).

So, to be a Christian believer is to be 'of the *truth*'. To live the Christian life aright is to do the *truth*, whereas the religious hypocrite 'walks in darkness and does not the *truth*' (*1 John* 1:6). The God of the Bible is the 'true God', and to have him is to have 'eternal life' (*1 John 5:20*). To know the *truth* is to believe that all other gods and all other gospels are 'idols' from which we must 'keep ourselves' (*1 John* 5:21).

It is essential that we pause to ask ourselves what is intended by this insistence by Jesus Christ on truth. In answer we say that it must mean just this: The only real world is that portrayed by the Bible. All other world-and-life views are false and invalid. They do not coincide with reality but are a kind of fantasy world. Those who reject the Bible's portrayal of existence are guilty of inventing a mythical, non-existent and therefore deceptive world. They live in a fool's paradise, a dream life which exists only in their own imagination and which will burst like a bubble once they pass beyond death into eternity. The sinner's imaginary world has no more of real existence than do the comic characters and cartoons of Disneyland.

When the Lord Jesus Christ informed Pilate that his mission in this world was to 'bear witness unto the truth' (*John* 18:37), he intended us to understand that the mission of the Christian church in every age is to challenge the false views of reality which exist in men's minds. It was this that Christ did in his own day. His sermons and miracles were a sharp challenge to the men of his generation, many of whom were very religious men in their own way. He considered it his mission to sweep away the cobwebs of superstition and tradition by which they had falsified reality and were distorting the rules of faith and duty for themselves and others. His view of reality differed essentially from that of the religious leaders of his day. His view was right, and theirs was wrong. The consequence was a profound clash and conflict between his view and theirs.

One might have supposed, had one lived two thousand years ago, that the existence of the Bible and the influence of the Christian church for so long would guarantee that most men would by this time have accepted the Christian world-and-life view. But it is not so. The natural man is profoundly offended by the Christian view of reality and, do what the church will, the unconverted world, so long as it remains unconverted, will always refuse to accept the true view of life. People in Christian countries are scarcely any more ready to look at life correctly today, after two millennia of gospel light, than their forefathers were in pre-Christian times. The distortion of reality may be less gross, but it is still there.

There cannot be any serious doubt in Christian minds today that the entire attitude and outlook to life which commonly prevails needs to be radically challenged. The thought patterns of men and women today, thanks to a century of declining Christianity in the West, are very far removed from those of the Bible. A score of competing philosophies, all of them far from truth, have taken possession of men's minds. The modern mind is obsessed with myths and errors like a cage full of unclean birds. What our time needs more than anything else is a fresh baptism of light and truth.

The religious, educational and cultural scene which meets our eye is one of fatigue and decadence. No greater proof or evidence is needed of the truth of the apostle's phrase: 'To be carnally minded is death' (*Rom.* 8:6) than what we all see around us. The intellectual life of modern society is stagnant. It runs in small and shallow channels. All the talk is about pleasure – especially sensual pleasure – and all the preoccupation is with commercial interests. Money, fashion, sport – and little else – are the socially correct topics of conversation. It is as if man's life consisted in nothing more important than what next to eat, what next to wear, where next to find a trivial pursuit.

Our society is ripe for a fresh injection of truth to lift us all above the cheapness of our age. We need it to live and breathe once more in the exciting realm of great and glorious thoughts – gospel thoughts. What truths they are! There are no facts to compare with those of the Bible! There are no ideas to match those of the gospel of Jesus Christ! They are exactly what our tired world needs to raise it from its bored preoccupation with every pleasure and to rouse the spirits of men to soar to lofty heights of thought and endeavour.

Gospel ideas, when they truly take hold of us, are electric in their potency. They grip the soul and mind as if with bands of iron, or adamantine steel. They galvanize the emotions into terrible waves of alarm and terror, till we are reconciled to the truth of them, till we come at last to acquiesce sweetly in them and eventually to bathe our souls in them with unutterable comfort. Truth is a furnace heated seven times hotter in which God places the souls of men till they emerge *new* men and have a new lustre in their hearts and on their faces.

Truth is an anvil upon which God places the conscience of men while he hammers them into a new shape. Let no one have small thoughts of truth. It is of God and comes from his very essence. All the truths of God are mighty, and in seasons of blessing they become incandescent. If any man doubts it, let him read Augustine's *Confessions* or Bunyan's *Grace Abounding*. Apart from the power of Christ's truth no man could ever begin to explain a Paul, or a Luther, or a Calvin or a Spurgeon. They were what they were because truth had laid hold of them and they had become its very slaves.

Oh! what havoc truth will wreak on society when next God is pleased to give it almighty power! Picture our modern society, so busily engaged in its routine of trivial pursuits, suddenly invaded by a powerful assault of gospel truths from heaven! Imagine the effect on hundreds and thousands of our dear fellow citizens of their being suddenly aroused and awakened by the great thoughts of the Bible: the wrath of God, the awfulness of everlasting punishment, the availability of Christ's blood for free pardon, the wicket gate still open to admit the penitent, the exquisite comfort of feeling the love of God poured upon the heart, the assuring witness of the Spirit of God in the innermost soul, the consoling hope of eternal bliss in a heavenly Father's home! These and similar truths are what won myriads in the far-off Roman Empire two millennia ago to throw their ancestral gods 'to the moles and to the bats' (*Isa.*2:20) and to venture their all on the promise of Christ to save them. It was, in Thomas Scott's phrase, 'the force of truth'.

We wish, with all the energy of our being, that the great God of truth would be pleased once again to visit the earth with a powerful invasion of his gospel truth. No blessing could remotely compare with it. No medicine could so perfectly cure our modern world of its many plagues. Signs and wonders will not do it, for men will not believe 'though one rose from the dead' (*Luke* 16:31). New and popular philosophies will not do it. The world had abundance of them before Christ came.

Ah! but *truth* will cure the ills of men. Let the gospel of a crucified Saviour be heard – 'not in word only, but also in power and in the Holy Ghost, and in much assurance' (*1 Thess.* 1:5) – and this sad modern world will have to sit up and take notice. It has happened in the past again and again and – pray God – will happen yet many times more when it is his pleasure to grant it to be so.

But who will preach this glorious gospel of truth to our perishing modern world? Latimer is gone; Whitefield is gone; Spurgeon and Lloyd-Jones are gone. Who then is to come?

O great God and Father of him who said, 'I am the truth', when wilt thou come and baptize thy church again with Pentecostal fire?

22

Justification: an Imperilled Doctrine

The most important issue facing all Christians of every church at this time is the vital one: How is a sinner justified before God? Various factors have, over the past few years, conspired to bring this, which is the greatest of all questions in religion, to the fore. In general, the Ecumenical Movement, with its insistence that all Christians should unite regardless of the claims of truth on the individual's conscience, has done so. The Second Vatican Council with its concessions to Protestants that they are not so much 'heretics' as 'separated brethren' has been another factor. More recently the move towards reunion with Rome of a large section of Lutheranism; the efforts at finding a common formula to unite Anglicans and Roman Catholics; and the Evangelicals and Catholics Together movement in the United States have all, in one way or another, brought to the forefront the need to seek fresh clarity on this central issue: How is a sinner justified before God?

Two essentially different answers to this question surfaced at the time of the Reformation, and they have divided the visible church in the West into Catholic and Protestant from that day to this. In its Council of Trent (1545–63), the Roman Catholic Church defined its doctrine of justification in this way. It affirmed, over against Protestantism, that justification consists of two things: 1. The infusion into the sinner of the quality of 'charity' (love), by which a sinner comes to seek God as his chief good; and 2. the forgiveness of sins. The first element here was regarded as the real essence of justification, while the second is a supplement to it. At the same time, the Lutheran/Calvinistic doctrine of justification was anathematized by the Council.

The Lutheran/Calvinistic, or Protestant, view stated that justification consists of the imputation of the righteousness of Christ to the sinner, by which he receives the forgiveness of his sins and is reckoned by God as righteous in Christ. The Protestant view denied that in justification there is any infusion of 'love' into the sinner and affirmed that justification is an act of imputation, not of infusion. The debate has centred on this point from the Reformation to the present day and shows no sign of abating. The Catholic and Protestant views of this subject are incompatible with one another. No formula will ever be found to reconcile them. Such formulas as have been offered to come to a compromise have sought to achieve peace either by sacrificing vital truth or else by offering an ambiguous pattern of words which each side can interpret in its own way. The real issue is this: in justification does God *impart* righteousness to man or does he *impute* righteousness to him?

The Catholic doctrine of justification is that of the great Augustine of Hippo (354–430). The Catholic Church over the thousand or so years from Augustine to Luther modified and developed its views on the doctrine of justification, but at the Reformation its basic attitude was that of Augustine. What did this Church Father teach on the subject of justification? Augustine's views on the justification of a sinner are expressed mainly in his writings against Pelagianism and semi-Pelagianism. At the Fall, man rebelled against God and became corrupt in nature, so that man now seeks his supreme good in created things rather than in the Creator himself.

What then, according to Augustine, is religious conversion? It is the grace of God acting on man in such a way that his fallen nature is 'replaced by grace'. This grace, he maintained, is bestowed on man at baptism. Those who fall from baptismal grace are restored through repentance. The Holy Spirit recreates man's heart and frees his enslaved will, thus enabling him to 'love' God and choose him as his chief good. This healing and renewing work in man's soul is variously termed by Augustine 'renovation', 'vivification', 'regeneration' and 'justification'. It is easy to find in his writings expressions which equate the healing 'righteousness' of God in the gospel with the renewal of man's nature.

Two excerpts from Augustine's writings may be given as examples of his thought on this subject:

1. Commenting on Romans 1:17, where Paul speaks of 'the righteousness of God', he says: 'He [Paul] does not say, the righteousness of man or the righteousness of his will, but the "righteousness of God" – meaning not that whereby he himself is righteous, but that with which he endows man when he justifies the ungodly . . .'

2. '"Being justified by his grace". It is not, therefore, by the law nor by their own will that they are justified; but they are justified freely by God's grace – not that the justification takes place without our will; but our will is shown to be weak by the law; that grace may heal its infirmity, and thus healed, it may fulfil the law' (*On the Spirit and Letter*, IX).

We leave aside here Augustine's obvious error of linking grace too closely to baptism. This mistake we may well believe with Warfield is one of those things which Augustine would have corrected had he lived long enough to work out fully his own evangelical doctrine of grace. It is clear that Augustine interpreted the New Testament doctrine of justification to include regeneration, or the sanctification of man's fallen nature. He is evangelical to the extent of denying to man's fallen will the power, apart from grace, to fulfil the law of God. He is not evangelical, however, in his understanding of 'the righteousness of God', which he construes as the righteousness of the renewed man himself and not the righteousness of Christ imputed to him.

Augustine's failure to expound accurately the doctrine of justification in the New Testament arose in part from his lack of proficiency in the Greek language. He failed to appreciate that *dikaioo* in Greek means to 'declare righteous' or 'acquit'. Since he read his New Testament mainly in Latin, he found there the term *iustificare* ('to *make* righteous'), and fell into the easy trap of defining justification in terms which are appropriate rather to the new birth and to sanctification.

This doctrine of justification as taught by Augustine became substantially the standard Catholic view. It was set out dogmatically by the Council of Trent at the time of the Reformation and has remained authoritative to this day. This is the doctrine still to be found in standard Catholic works such as the *Catechism of the Catholic Church,* the Latin text of which received its imprimatur from Cardinal Joseph Ratzinger as recently as 1994. In this authoritative *Catechism* justification, as in Augustine, has the two elements of renewal and forgiveness: 'Moved by grace, man turns toward God and away from sin, thus accepting forgiveness and righteousness from on high' (*Catholic Catechism,* para. 1989). The Council of Trent's earlier words are here affirmed by the *Catechism:* 'Justification is not only the remission of sins, but also the sanctification and renewal of the interior man' (*ibid.*). Again, 'By giving birth to the "inner man", justification entails the *sanctification* of his whole being' (para. 1995). The element of baptismal grace is as present in the modern *Catechism* as ever: 'Our justification comes from the grace of God . . . Grace is a *participation in the life of God.* It introduces us into the intimacy of Trinitarian life: by baptism the Christian participates in the grace of Christ, the Head of his Body' (paras. 1996, 1997). The old concept of 'merit' is also present: 'Moved by the Holy Spirit and by charity, *we can then merit* for ourselves and for others the graces needed for our sanctification . . . and for the attainment of eternal life' (para. 2010).

It was this view of justification which Martin Luther learned from the Catholic Church of his day and which prior to his famous 'Tower experience', probably at the end of 1518, he believed and taught in his lectures. The mature Luther, however, following his experience in the 'Tower', held and taught a doctrine of justification which departs radically from Augustine and from Rome. The following quotations from his writings will illustrate how significantly Luther's views differed from those of his early upbringing:

1. 'Your righteousness is Christ, who was made a curse for you and who redeemed you from the curse of the law' (On *Gal.* 4:27).

2. 'The fruit and benefit of his [Christ's] sacrifice and ministry are the forgiveness of sins and justification' (*Church Postil*, Fifth Sunday in Lent).

3. 'Our righteousness is nothing but imputation.' 'It consists not in any merits, but in the favour and imputation of God through faith' (*Bondage of the Will*).

4. 'Man is justified when he appropriates and receives by faith this forgiveness of imputed righteousness. Faith does not justify because it is a new quality in man, but because it lays hold of the promise of grace and relies on the mercy of God alone.' 'We are justified by faith alone, because faith alone appropriates the victory of Christ' (On *Gal.* 3:13).

5. 'Justification does not take place through works, but by faith alone, without any works . . . completely and at once. Truly it is plain, then, that faith alone brings such good things of God, that is, justification and salvation, and makes us instantaneously, not gradually, children and heirs, who then freely do good works of all kinds' (On *Gal.* 4:5).

The respects in which Luther's doctrine of justification differs from Augustine's are in that 1. the 'righteousness' of a justified man, according to Luther, is wholly and entirely Christ's righteousness; 2. it is a 'righteousness' in which the good deeds of a renewed sinner play no part; 3. it is a 'righteousness' received by faith alone; 4. it is a 'righteousness' which confers immediate acceptance with God; 5. it is a 'righteousness' which brings him assurance and joy in spite of his remaining imperfections of heart and life.

It is not to be thought that Luther had no place in his thinking for a divine renewal of the heart. Luther believed in spiritual renewal just as Augustine had done. But this work of renewal, he argued, must be most clearly distinguished from justification properly so called. He sometimes refers to 'first justification' and 'second justification', the first being the imputation of Christ's righteousness to the believing sinner and the second the renewal of his nature in what is now normally termed sanctification.

The relationship between these two is taken up by Luther in his academic disputations held at Wittenburg from 1536 to 1543. For example, he states the difference in this way: 'For he first cleanses by imputation, then (*deinde*) he gives the Holy Spirit, by whom we are cleansed in regard to our substance. Faith purifies through the remission of sins; the Holy Spirit purifies by his effect' (*Disputations of Justification*, 1536).

The light which, by God's grace, Luther threw on the doctrine of justification is reflected in all the Reformation confessions, both Continental and British. Luther's doctrine was recognized by all the Reformers and their successors to be that of Paul and of the Holy Scriptures. They agreed with the great German Reformer that this one point of doctrine is all-important to the well-being, and indeed to the very being, of any professing church of Christ.

The Protestant doctrine from Luther's day onward is that expressed in the words, for instance, of the Westminster *Larger Catechism* of 1648:

'Justification is an act of God's free grace unto sinners, in which He pardoneth all their sins, accepteth and accounteth their persons righteous in His sight, not for any thing wrought in them, or done by them, but only for the perfect obedience and full satisfaction of Christ, by God imputed to them, and received by faith alone.'

It became necessary from the time of the Reformation onwards in any Protestant definition of justification, not only to *affirm* the positive elements but also to *deny* those Augustinian and Catholic elements which from Luther's time onward were deemed to have no place in our justification as sinners.

How did Luther come to recognize the true meaning of 'righteousness' and of a sinner's justification before God? If we take the Luther scholar, Dr Uuras Saarnivaara, as our guide, we should appreciate that Luther's teaching on justification 'was closely connected with the deepening of his conception of sin' (*Luther Discovers the Gospel*, p. 113). The more he became acquainted, especially in the years following 1512, with the Bible and with the depravity of his own heart, the more clearly he saw the utter impossibility of securing a standing before God based on any works of his own. Even as a Christian his best works, so far from earning 'merit' before God, were 'filthy rags'. In the years 1518 to 1521, Luther advocated this aspect of man's justification repeatedly. (Luther had a truly biblical view of justification only in and after the year 1518. 'Young' Luther was not yet a Reformer.)

Luther's 'Tower experience' (dated by Saarnivaara at the end of 1518) did not occur in a vacuum. From 1513 and onwards he had been giving academic lectures to students at Wittenburg and had an 'unusually ardent desire', he informs us, 'to understand Paul in his Epistle to the Romans'. Yet he there found a problem: 'In spite of the ardour of my heart I was hindered by the unique word in the first chapter, "the righteousness of God is revealed in it". I hated that word "righteousness of God", because . . . I had been taught to understand it philosophically as meaning . . . the formal or active righteousness according to which God is righteous and punishes sinners . . .'

'Day and night I tried to meditate upon the significance of these words: "The righteousness of God is revealed in it, as it is written, The righteous shall live by faith". Then finally', says Luther, 'God had mercy on me, and I began to understand that the righteousness of God is that gift of God by which a righteous man lives, namely faith, and that this sentence "The righteousness of God is revealed in the gospel" is passive . . . Now I felt as though I had been reborn altogether and had entered Paradise. In the same moment the face of the whole of Scripture became apparent to me.'

In this one experience the Reformation was born. More than a thousand years of misunderstanding was rolled back. The imperfect definition of justification offered by Augustine was subjected to biblical correction. Paul's authentic doctrine now dawned on the soul of the German monk. Before long the world was to be turned upside down by it.

We began by asserting that the most important issue facing Christians everywhere today is that of how the sinner is justified before God. Almost half a millennium has run its course since Luther's evangelical discovery in the 'Tower' at Wittenburg. But the value of his discovery is as great for the church of Christ as the day he made it. A clear understanding of God's method of justification was lost to the church for over a thousand years.

A great many voices Catholic and 'Protestant', are today being raised against the Lutheran and Pauline doctrine in the professing church of Christ. The future must ever remain hidden from our eyes but, should the biblical doctrine of justification – may God forbid! – be lost to the world again, its loss could only spell bondage and misery to millions of souls. Certain it is in every age that where there is no justification there is no joy, no hope and no gospel.

Who then will champion this truth in our times?

23

'The Spirits in Prison'

The Bible is the first and most essential means of grace. Our worship and prayer is only acceptable in the measure in which it is regulated by the teaching of the Bible. Well-intentioned sincerity is a valuable thing, but it will not make our worship pleasing to God if it is not regulated by his Word. It is a thousand pities to see well-meaning persons attempting to worship and serve God devotely but in a way not sanctioned by his Word. Our worship is worthless unless it is offered to God in accordance with his own revealed will.

Exactly the same is true of our confession or creed. We believe in vain any doctrine which the Bible has not revealed to us. Belief in any doctrine which is not from God is only misbelief. Our life-long calling as Christians is to remove from our hearts and lives all doctrines and practices which do not have the warrant or sanction of God's Word and are therefore inconsistent with his Word. To believe any falsehood to be true, or any truth to be false, is harmful to our faith and hurtful to our souls.

It follows from what has been said that we must all be careful and life-long students of the Bible. We must constantly correct our beliefs and practices against the teaching of the Word of God, even if at times such correction and reformation may be painful. All reformation of faith and worship, doctrine and practice *is* painful because it cuts across our fond and cherished attitudes of mind and our familiar patterns of belief and devotion. But reformation is the believer's duty.

It sometimes happens, however, that men's false ideas in matters of faith and devotion are actually derived from the Bible itself, or rather, from hasty and ill-considered interpretations of it. Examples of this abound, the most notorious being related to the words of Christ, 'This is my body.'

It is not enough therefore that our faith be loosely related to the words of the Bible. What is required of us all is to study the Bible till we have understood its true and proper *sense*. It is the *meaning* and the *message* of Scripture which form the substance of what we are to believe. Each particular text of the Bible is capable of being misunderstood. Many, according to the Apostle Peter, wrest the Scripture 'unto their own destruction' (*2 Pet.* 3:16). To be biblical is to be governed by the true meaning and interpretation of Scripture. False interpretations always lead astray from Christ. And some texts, it has to be admitted, present us with serious problems of interpretation.

Just such a passage of Scripture is to be found in 1 Peter 3:18–20: 'For Christ also hath once suffered for sins, the just for the unjust, that he might bring us to God, being put to death in the flesh, but quickened by the Spirit: By which also he went and preached unto the spirits in prison; Which sometime were disobedient, when once the long-suffering of God waited in the days of Noah, while the ark was a preparing, wherein few, that is, eight souls were saved by water.' This text has truly been a 'dismal swamp' to Bible readers. Even some commentators of real worth have stumbled over the meaning of these words and attempted to draw harmful conclusions from them. It will be profitable for us to come to a clear and settled view of the meaning of this difficult passage.

SOME WRONG VIEWS

It is a common mistake of commentators to start out with the assumption that Christ 'went and preached unto the spirits in prison' (verse 19) during the period between his death and resurrection. This is a regrettable, if partly understandable, mistake and one that leads to some mischievous doctrines. Commentators who try to interpret the text in this way are influenced by the nearby words which state that Christ was 'put to death in the flesh, but quickened by the Spirit' (verse 18). They perhaps assume that the preaching of our Lord here must have taken place during the time between his being put to death and his being quickened by the Spirit.

To interpret Peter's words in this way, however, quickly lands us in trouble. Who are these spirits and in what prison are they? Those who embark on this method of interpretation are faced with various possible answers to these questions. The spirits could be either fallen angels (and demons), or the souls of the damned in hell, or else the souls of Old Testament saints in Hades, conceived of as the 'waiting room' for them till Christ should come. We suppose that there might be found advocates for each of these various views.

But if this line of interpretation is correct in the main, what is Christ supposed to have preached to them at that time when he himself was disembodied and in a state of death? The 'kindest' view is that our Lord entered the place where the souls of Old Testament saints were at rest and announced to them that his work was now completed on the Cross. They might now leave Hades and rise to heaven.

The 'grimmest' view is that our Lord entered into the dark vaults of hell and there announced that the doom of the wicked, both demons and men, was now sealed forever in that he had triumphed over Satan and thus ensured that the wicked would never escape. This view, so the writer once heard, has been referred to as 'the harrowing of hell'. It was, if this view is correct, a gloomy preaching indeed which these spirits received.

There is, however, one very good reason for believing that this entire method of interpretation is wrong and misleading. It is the statement of Christ to the thief on the cross, 'Today shalt thou be with me in paradise' (*Luke* 23:43). Here we are informed that Christ's soul in a state of death was in the place of the blessed dead and nowhere else. If so, he was not in hell. And he was not in some 'waiting room' but in the place where the Old Testament saints, though disembodied, were in comfort and at peace, like Abraham and Lazarus (*Luke* 16:23, 25).

A second consideration which ought to make us very reluctant to follow the interpretation of those commentators referred to above is that preaching is a spiritual exercise confined entirely to this present life. The Bible knows of no preaching to the dead, either to the blessed dead or to the wicked. Singing is certainly heard in heaven, but not preaching. Still less is there any preaching to those in hell. It is inconsistent with all that we are told about heaven or hell to suppose that preaching is ever heard in either place. Preaching is a means of grace to men while they are still in a state of probation in this present life. Once our spiritual condition is sealed by death we are beyond all possibility of change. If so, then preaching would be of no value at all, for preaching aims to change men.

A serious evil flowing from the adoption of the interpretation above is that room must be found for some such place as purgatory. As a matter of fact this whole passage has been used to attempt to prove that a purgatory of some sort exists and that Christ descended into hell after his death.[1] Thus interpreted, Peter's words are the gateway to superstition.

Towards a Right Understanding

The materials needed to help us towards a correct interpretation are all in the Bible and some of them are even in the context of this very passage itself. One key to unlock the meaning is found in these words of Peter's a few verses later: 'For for this cause was the gospel preached also to them that are dead, that they might be judged according to men in the flesh, but live according to God in the spirit' (*1 Pet.*

---

[1] For instance, the *Catechism of the Catholic Church* adduces 1 Peter 3:18–19 to prove that Christ, the place of the dead and preached the Good News to the spirits imprisoned there (Articles, para. 632)

4:6). The background to Peter's thought is the imminence of the judgment day. Of great importance is the way in which he refers to the dead: 'The gospel *was* preached to them that *are* dead.' The persons referred to *are* now dead but the gospel *was* preached to them while they were alive.

The exact same sense is to be attached to 1 Peter 3:19: 'He (Christ) . . . went and preached to the spirits in prison.' These spirits, or souls of men now disembodied in a state of death, had the gospel preached to them while they were alive on earth. If we were to expand, or paraphrase, this verse we should have to be careful how we did it: 'Christ went and preached to the spirits who *are now*, not *were*, in prison.'

It is of interest to know that the Latin Vulgate Bible, in use during the Middle Ages, translated *'were'* in prison (*erant*), whereas the Reformer Theodore Beza, friend of Calvin, translated it *'are'* in prison (*sunt*). The Vulgate translation has led to a good deal of needless confusion over this text. Peter is not saying that Christ preached to those who *were* dead, but to those who *are now* dead. They were alive when Christ preached to them but they are not alive now.[1]

OTHER PROBLEMS

What precisely are these 'spirits in prison'? They are the disembodied souls of those evil men who heard and rejected the preaching of Christ and so are now in the intermediate state of hell. The full and final state of heaven and hell are not yet manifested by God. The souls of the righteous are in

---

[1] Those who wish to have a convenient survey of these confused views should consult such a technical commentary on First Peter as that of E. G. Selwyn (Macmillan, 1969).

glory but they still await the return of Christ to enjoy the ultimate and final state of heaven. Similarly, the wicked dead are not yet in the final state of hell as it is to be opened up after the Day of Judgment. They are at present kept in a place of suffering and confinement, as in a prison, till the Judgment Day. Hence, they are here aptly described as 'spirits in prison'. They are, of course, human beings, not demons. The gospel has never at any period of history been preached to demons, who have no Saviour, and so no hope.

But when and how did our blessed Saviour Jesus Christ preach to these spirits? He did so at the time before the Flood of Noah's day, 'while the ark was a preparing' (verse 20). It is clear therefore that the reference is not to any preaching of Christ during his earthly life or ministry, or to any mysterious ministry of preaching carried out by him between his death and resurrection. This reference is to the preaching of Christ in his pre-incarnate state 'in the days of Noah' (verse 20).

How then did Christ preach during the one hundred and twenty years when the ark was being built by Noah? He did so by his Holy Spirit given by him to Noah, who was an inspired mouth-piece for Christ, warning the pleasure-loving sinners of that age to flee from the impending wrath of God by repenting and entering the ark. Hence Peter affirms that Christ was 'quickened' (made alive, at his resurrection) by *the Spirit* (verse 18). The same Holy Spirit who raised up Christ from the dead (*Rom.* 8:11) also inspired Noah to preach in those far-off antediluvian times 'when once the long-suffering of God waited' (verse 20).

How then is it here said that Christ '*went* and preached unto the spirits in prison' (verse 19)? The verb 'went' must refer to gracious divine action on Christ's part and not to physical movement. Christ in his rich grace gave an abundance of his Spirit to Noah, whom Peter elsewhere refers to as 'a preacher of righteousness' (*2 Pet.* 2:5).

This would indicate that the preaching which the men at the Flood heard from the lips of Noah was no ordinary preaching but was an anointed, gracious, Christ-given preaching. And yet, for all that, those who heard it were impenitent to the last. Noah's preaching, Spirit-filled and Christ-given as it was, saved not a single man outside his own family. This fact must be a comfort to many a modern preacher and missionary who is too honest to falsify facts.

The judgment which came down upon these impenitent men of Noah's day, as all know, was in the form of a deluge of water (verse 20). Peter, however, does not draw our attention to the flood waters as the instrument of God's wrath. Rather, he asserts that the eight who entered the ark were saved by water. The very element which destroyed the impenitent saved those who obeyed God at that time. In the economy of God it is often, perhaps always, so. One means in God's hand spells life to believers and death to the scornful, whether that means be the waters of the Flood, the Red Sea or the last great fire. This fire will burn up this sinful world's corrupt works and at the same time usher in a purified universe for the people of God.

Peter expands on the significance of the element of water to teach us the importance of baptism. The same element which lifted up the ark and its occupants to safety above the raging waves in Noah's day is now used by God to save us (verse 21). He hastens to dispel any misconception on this point. The water does not save us, he explains, by automatic contact with our skin like some external washing, but when it is the sacramental symbol of an internal cleansing by which we are able to look up to a holy God with love and faith – our conscience reassuring us of justification in Christ.

The main pastoral problem evidently addressed by Peter in this whole First Epistle is that of the sufferings of God's people in this unkind world. To this theme he turns again and again in the course of the epistle.

PETER'S MESSAGE TO BELIEVERS

It remains to explain how the passage we have here been explaining and expounding is related to the general theme of the epistle as a whole. This we must now do.

In this world the Christian must expect to suffer many injustices. He will therefore have to suffer even for *well-doing* (verse 17), an experience which is especially hard for the human spirit to bear because it feels so unjust. But an argument is at hand to help us to bear even this, 'for Christ also hath once suffered for sins, the just for the unjust' (verse 18). If we remember that our Master so suffered, it is vastly easier for us to suffer injustice in this world.

Besides, Christ and his people have in the various ages of human history, all had to go through the same experiences of suffering unjustly. Yet both he and they have always finally triumphed over the ills of this life and been saved out of them at last. Noah and his family saw evils in plenty in their day. But they were saved out of them at length by those very waters which destroyed the sinners who rejected Christ's gospel.

The water of baptism – provided it be baptism indeed, associated with a renewed soul and so with a quickened and good conscience – now saves us just as surely as it saved Noah of old. As he rose above this world's troubles in the ark so shall we also in the end of our life. This assurance is fortified by the further fact that Christ, who suffered for well-doing in this life, is now both risen and ascended to his glory above. It cannot be long therefore till we join our beloved Saviour in his glory.

The Christian living in this new millennium and seeing all round him the same evils that Noah saw and the same ominous contempt for the gospel, should take fresh heart. If we are faithful to Christ we shall not fail to appear with him at last in glory.

24

The History of Unbelief

The chief and leader of all the sins which men commit is unbelief. It is the essence of all sins. It is the very distillation of sin. It is an unpardonable sin in that, wherever it reigns fully in the soul, a man cannot be saved. Unbelief is the father of sins and is found in every sin. It is the hardest sin to master and the last to be mortified. It follows all men from the cradle to the grave. No Christian is free from its chilling influence. It is the spirit of the world. It knows no shame, but scorns God, pours doubt upon truth, denies all that Christ has said or done, scoffs at goodness and turns love to poison.

The happiness and comfort of men and nations rises or else falls in proportion as they are able to conquer unbelief. Where unbelief rules all institutions disintegrate and die: the family, marriage, civil government, neighbourliness, the church, the school, the law-court. Unbelief is the needle which draws after it the long thread of woes which plague mankind: atheism, fear, anxiety, anarchy, crime and despair.

Happy is the man who mounts above this pestilence and happy the nation which rises above it. It will be part of the blessedness of those who get to heaven that they will there be at last entirely freed from the cold touch of unbelief. There at length they will know that *all* God's words are true and faithful. The wicked in hell, sadly, will spend a long eternity regretting that all the joys of heaven were forfeited by them only through unbelief.

Not the least part of the evil of unbelief is its cunning craftiness. It walks in all disguises. It wears all names: 'maturity', 'broad-mindedness', 'learning', 'scholarship'. It is found in universities, in king's palaces, in temples and in the cottages of the poor. It smiles on religion as on some sickly child about to die. It is confident before microphones and never misses a chance to appear on stage and screen. Unbelief is the one great actor who never dies. Other actors and actresses come and go. They have their exits and their entrances. But unbelief outlives them all. She looks down greedily on each rising generation, sings to them her lullabies, rapes their consciences with her easy morals and even sings the hymn at their funeral service. Her last sermon is: 'Our friend was no believer. But he is at peace like others.'

The Bible is the history of unbelief. She was born in heaven in the heart of the angel Lucifer and was not slow to migrate to the Garden of Eden where she found a congenial welcome. She escorted our first parents out of their first home and became tutor to their eldest son, whom she educated in the art of fratricide. Her maturing years, like her childhood, have been marked by thorough consistency of character. She successfully dissuaded the 'happy' generation at the time of the Flood from being so absurd as to enter Noah's ark. She laughed with the gay age in Sodom. She has never believed in anything so fanatical as Jonah and the whale, or in hell, or in an inerrant Bible. Having a broad-minded tolerance of tradition and of all human goodness, she helped Israel in Old Testament times to avoid a too scrupulous adherence to any prescribed creed or form of worship, however inspired. And when Christ at last appeared she used all her powers of logic to convince both Herod, Pontius Pilate and the Sanhedrin that it was 'expedient ... that one man should die for the people, and that the whole nation perish not' (*John* 11:50).

Unbelief, if we are to go by the most reliable reports, has not been idle in New Testament times. She has made a healthy use of experience gained in former ages and has devoted her time to a specialist study of the Christian Church, which she has striven untiringly to keep from all extremes of faith or obedience to God. When she could, after the time of Constantine, no longer keep men away from Christianity by fire, sword or wild beasts, she became expert in re-writing the Christian creed, bit by bit, till mankind, under her tuition, even discovered how to make Christ out of a piece of bread. She taught our medieval forefathers how to pardon sins for money and deny all articles of the faith while professing to believe them.

Unbelief had successful campaigns in Europe in the late nineteenth century. As an evangelist for her own forms of theology she conducted excellent crusades, first in German universities and then elsewhere. She turned many scholars to her 'very reasonable' views of religion and morality at the turn of the century. Since then she has published her distinctive doctrines widely also in Britain and America, once bastions of a conservatism which she thoroughly disapproved of. Indeed, the West generally has taken wholesale to her fashionable teachings. The relaxed attitude to everything good, bad and indifferent is one by-product of her extensive educational policy worldwide.

One embarrassing problem with unbelief is that it comes in where it is most unwelcome – even into our own hearts and lives as Christians. It knows no respect for orthodoxy but enters in through the door into Reformed churches quite as easily as into Arminian assemblies. Unbelief is the arch-reformer who never wearies of pleading for change. Whether the church be Baptist or Brethren, Presbyterian or Anglican, her voice is sooner or later heard at the church meeting. She will want to 'improve' on everything and to secure for all churches the blessing of being 'less severe', 'less forbidding', 'more comfortable'. Unbelief is always coyly on the look-out for willing friends who will say a good word for her cause in church circles. Her maxim is: 'If you say a thing often enough, some will eventually believe you.' In this she shows her knowledge of our weakness.

The best cure for unbelief is to look at the life and teaching of the One Man in all history who was never put off by it. Jesus Christ alone of all mankind rose perfectly above it. His whole ministry was one long attack on the evil of unbelief. He exposed it for the monster that it is and took away its mask that we might recognize the face behind it. He allowed unbelief to alter neither his message nor his ministry of mercy to sinners.

Unbelief, if we listen to Christ, is man's sworn and mortal enemy. Every blessing that God bestows comes to us by faith. By faith we understand that the universe was created by God's almighty power. By faith we see that not a sparrow falls to the ground without the knowledge of the Heavenly Father. By faith we enter God's Kingdom. By faith we are kept in it. By faith we pray and work, fight and watch, preach and serve, live and die aright. By faith 'all things are possible' to us (*Mark* 9:23). Faith is the cure for worry, fear, doubt, despair and a thousand other evils that beset our life here in this world. So Christ taught in his ministry, both in private and in public. Christ's was, in the truest possible sense, a 'faith mission' to our unhappy world.

Our Saviour's finger pointed always to unbelief as our deepest problem. He did not come crusading for 'temperance', or for 'equality' or for some other desirable social improvement. At least, he did not do so *directly*. He did not strike at the branches of sin but went to the root – to the sin of doubt, from which all evils flow.

The Christian life, correctly understood, is wholly a life of faith. The new birth is essential (*John* 3:3) because without it a man *cannot* believe and *cannot* come to Christ (*John* 6:35). The whole Christian life is closed to a man or woman who lacks faith. They no more know what it means to know and love God than a blind man knows what we mean by the beautiful sheen on the petal of a rose, or on the wing of a bird.

The soul begins its spiritual life with God the moment it passes from unbelief to faith. In that instant it travels a spiritual distance greater than that between the North and

South Poles. It is 'delivered from the power of darkness and translated into the kingdom of God's dear Son' (*Col.* 1:13). The visible alteration which we see in a man's life after this mighty change is in the way he now lives by faith. All our progress in grace as believers is closely related to our progress in faith. Faith is the index of the new-born soul and all its experiences, both high and low, reflect the measure and the exercise of faith within the hidden man of the heart.

The Christian's greatest need is to believe more than he does. We believe in an inspired Bible, but we need to believe it more than we do. We believe in the providence of God; we need to believe it still more. We believe in the Holy Spirit; we have need of more faith in him still. We believe in the gospel as the power of God; we have not believed yet as we should. We believe in the leading and guidance of God for our lives; we have need to believe and trust much more.

One fruitful study in our Bibles is: The ways in which men of faith were lacking in faith. We would not wish to study the theme so as to draw attention to *their* weakness so much as to *ours*. Abraham's faith failed in the matter of Sarah's beauty when they had to go to a pagan land (*Gen.* 12:11–13). Yet God was faithful to them both when the test came (verse 17). Rebekah's faith in God's oracle failed when she heard Isaac promise the blessing to Esau (*Gen.* 27:4). Yet God's word came exactly to pass to all who were concerned. Oh, that good men of whom we read in God's Word had only believed more fully! The lives of David, Solomon, Peter and others would then have been still more full of heavenly lustre than they were. O David, how could you begin to doubt God when pursued by Saul (*1 Sam.* 27:1)? O Peter, how could your faith fail as you walked to Christ on the waters of Galilee (*Matt.* 14:30–31)? The answer is that their faith, though strong, was liable to ebb and flow. By faith they did good and great things for God; by unbelief they left a record to us of the frailty of men, even the very best.

Our rich comfort when studying the failure of good men's faith is to notice that God never failed them. 'If we believe not, yet he abideth faithful' (*2 Tim.* 2:13). The great mercy, even in our failure of faith, is that God 'cannot deny himself' (*2 Tim.* 2:13). The mercies of the Lord towards those who are in covenant with him are unfailing and eternal.

The history of unbelief will have its last chapter when Christ comes again. It will go with those who love it and promote it into the 'lake of fire' (*Rev.* 20:15) along with the devil and his angels. The children of faith will at last have the victory over all the powers of doubt and darkness. Our hearts will be always restless until they rest on the Word of God. Every effort therefore must be directed towards getting and keeping them there. For Jesus every question and doubt was resolved by these words: It is *written!*

THE HOPE OF GLORY
– THE SECOND COMING
AND HEAVEN

25

The Believer's Half-Life

I f, as Christians, we could read life from the end backwards, we should all be much happier than we are. We can do this with the saints in the Bible, and we count them blessed because they all come to their happy ending. The patriarchs had to go through their lonely wanderings, but in the end they all got to the 'better country' (*Heb.* 11:16). The heroes of faith went 'through fire and water', but at length God brought them to a 'wealthy place' (*Psa.* 66:12). The prophets too, after delivering their heavy burden of prophecy and pronouncing their inspired oracles, all passed over to their place of rest. Like Daniel, they finished their course and stood 'in their lot at the end of the days' (*Dan.* 12:13). The Old Testament saints got safely home, and so, when we read of their many sufferings, we feel comfort for them because we know the end of their history and we remember that 'their latter end is peace' (*Psa.* 37:37).

The same is true of the great New Testament heroes. Peter, Paul and the other choice servants of Jesus Christ each drank of Christ's cup of affliction and shared in his baptism of sorrows in the course of their ministries (*Matt.* 20:23). But the end of their sufferings was triumphant. They had an 'abundant entrance into the everlasting kingdom of our Lord and Saviour Jesus Christ' (*2 Pet.* 1:11). They got to the place where there are no more imprisonments, no more stonings, no more shipwrecks, no more rivalry of false apostles, no more contending with 'unreasonable men who have not faith' (*2 Thess.* 3:2).

The believer's life is a type of parabola in which the curve first goes down, but then goes up again at last. All God's people, more or less, have to go through this parabola experience. It is the life-pattern of God's elect. They first suffer with Christ, and then they reign with him (*2 Tim*. 2:12).

The pattern is seen in the life of our blessed Saviour himself. He expresses this fact to his own disciples in this way: 'Ought not Christ to have suffered these things, and to enter into his glory?' (*Luke* 24:26). Peter's way of stating the same truth concerning Christ is in the words 'the sufferings of Christ, and the glory that should follow' (*1 Pet.* 1:11). James likewise explains this parabola experience in this way: 'Take, my brethren, the prophets, who have spoken in the name of the Lord, for an example of suffering affliction, and of patience. Behold we count them happy which endure. Ye have heard of the patience of Job, and have seen the end of the Lord; that the Lord is very pitiful, and of tender mercy' (*James* 5:10–11). Similarly, Paul declares that 'the sufferings of this present time are not worthy to be compared with the glory which shall be revealed in us' (*Rom.* 8:18). Christ and his people have a state of humiliation before they arrive at their state of exaltation.

The problem with us as Christians is that we regularly forget the last chapter of our life because we cannot yet read it. If we could read the last chapter of life and then see our present miseries in the light of it we should 'rejoice in the Lord alway' (*Phil.* 4:4). The secret of present happiness is to see our life as a *whole* and not merely to see it a page at a time.

Most worldly people read life page by page. They learn very little from the earlier chapters of their life. Even at the personal level it is generally true that 'history teaches that history teaches nothing' to worldly people. Above all, they live almost completely ignorant of the final chapter of life. The way of the world is to snatch life's pleasures while one can, to gather life's honey in youth, and to close one's eyes to morose old age and the cruel grave – unwelcome but inevitable – till they at last inexorably arrive.

On the other hand, when the Christian is unhappy or depressed, it is surely because, unless ill, he has forgotten his happy ending. He is allowing present problems to obscure his assured hope. His bright prospects are presently eclipsed. But they will appear again before too long. And the sooner he remembers that he is to 'live happily ever after', the sooner his sadness will disperse.

The common mistake of us all, as Christians, is to look at only '*half*' of our life, the 'half' we have lived through and not the 'half' we are yet to have. Scientists who study radioactive matter refer to its 'half-life'. Christians too have their 'half-life'. It is that part which they look back over with the passing of the years. But this is only the first 'half'. The best 'half' is still to come. 'Our light affliction, which is but for a moment, worketh for us a far more exceeding and eternal weight of glory' (*2 Cor.* 4:17). The painful first 'half' of a believer's life is but a 'moment' in length. His 'last chapter' is to last eternally, and it is to be written in letters of gold. It is to have a 'weight of glory' all over it and all through it. Oh, if only we could keep it squarely in view!

If the Christian is to live above his fears and above his feelings, he must learn the art of seeing his life in the light of its last chapter. Well did a good old Puritan say, 'He who rides to be crowned cares not about the rain.' We are riding to be crowned with Christ. We ride on the King's Highway towards privileges which beggar all our thoughts. If our path is rough and the weather rainy, it cannot spoil our hope of sitting on Christ's throne at last, of 'judging angels' (*1 Cor.* 6:3), of 'seeing God' (*Matt.* 5:8) and of walking with Christ 'in white' (*Rev.* 7:9).

There are good and wise reasons why the God who predestinates his elect to such mega-blessings as the above should see fit to put them in this life through such varied and harsh trials on the way to them. No comfort is like the comfort that comes after trouble, and no rest is like the rest we have after toil. So will the saint's everlasting rest be to him when he gets to the end of them all and falls asleep in Jesus. 'He shall enter into peace: they shall rest in their beds, each one walking in his uprightness' (*Isa.* 57:2).

Though for a short season Rachel must weep for her children as they pass through the valley of the shadow of death here below, she will at last know why the Lord has said, 'Refrain thy voice from weeping, and thine eyes from tears: for thy work shall be rewarded . . . And there is hope in thine end, saith the Lord, that thy children shall come again to their own border' (*Jer.* 31: 16-17).

When Job said to his wife, 'Shall we receive good at the hand of God, and shall we not receive evil?' (*Job* 2:10), he was still ignorant of the good which the Lord planned to do him in this life. He spoke by faith, knowing that God can do us more good by our sufferings and miseries than by our outward blessings. Job's miseries and sufferings had still to intensify before he got his eventual comfort, but his soul retained its grasp of the moral purpose in a believer's afflictions: 'But he knoweth the way that I take: when he hath tried me, I shall come forth as gold' (*Job 23:10*).

It is not an accident that spiritual eminence is closely related to sanctified affliction. God sharpens our souls on the grind-stone of pain and disappointment. Joseph's feet were in fetters; the iron went into his soul (*Psa.* 105:18). These experiences were preparatory to his later eminent service to God and to his generation. Hannah's early disappointment served the same moral purpose. When God later dried her eyes, she saw a divinely-wise method in God's dealings: 'The LORD killeth and maketh alive: he bringeth down to the grave, and bringeth up. The LORD maketh poor, and maketh rich: he bringeth low, and lifteth up. He raiseth up the poor out of the dust, and lifteth up the beggar from the dunghill, to set them among princes, and to make them inherit the throne of glory' (*1 Sam.* 2:6-8).

God puts a thorn in the believer's nest to teach him how to fly upwards on the wing of prayer. Those who have little affliction have little prayer. The false and easy-going Christian prays like a parrot. His prayer begins in his throat. But the true Christian's prayer rises out of the depths of his soul. It is hot, volcanic and like lava. His prayers to God are super-heated by his trials. And they move mountains.

It is the method of Christ's preaching and of the apostles to remind their believing hearers of their second 'half-life'. We see the Saviour on the eve of his departure and of their world mission assuring them of their place in the everlasting 'mansions' at last (*John* 14:2). Similarly, Paul comforts the Thessalonians in their persecutions with this glad prospect: 'It is a righteous thing with God to recompense tribulation to them that trouble you; And to you who are troubled rest with us, when the Lord Jesus shall be revealed from heaven with his mighty angels' (*2 Thess.* 1:6–7). In the same way Peter lifts the eyes of the soon-to-be martyred believers of the Roman Empire to survey their unfading 'inheritance', shortly to be conferred upon them at the appearance of Jesus Christ (*1 Pet.* 1:4).

The wrong way to live the Christian life is to look at the things which we now see, feel and suffer. Those who pity Christians because they have a bitter first 'half-life' do not see the crown of glory which they will shortly wear. The man who has a 'this-life-only' mentality will understandably discard the Christian faith at once as a bad bargain. 'If in this life only we have hope in Christ, we are of all men most miserable' (*1 Cor.* 15:19). But this is a false assumption. There is to be a sounding of the great trumpet of God. There is to be a resurrection to eternal glory. The believer's sufferings and labours for Christ are not 'in vain' (*1 Cor.* 15:58).

In God's glorious and good providence there is a correspondence between the first and second half of a believer's life. Moses saw it to be so all those many centuries ago: 'Make us glad *according to* the days wherein thou hast afflicted us, and the years wherein we have seen evil' (*Psa.* 90:15). The trials and tribulations of the 'first half' of our life are to be proportionately balanced by a comfort and a rest which correspond to them. Billy Bray knew it well when he exclaimed, 'God has given me sorrow with a tea-spoon but comfort and joy with a ladle.'

26

Entering into Rest

However good the worldly man imagines his life to be, it is a life which can only get worse and worse. Good health cannot last forever. The appetites will decline with age. The inevitable process of physical deterioration must rob the man of the world of at least half the quality of his life, as he once knew it in his youth. If his life is long it is also clouded with cares for his own health and that of others in his circle who are ageing with him. However much he consoles himself with memories of the past, he cannot now entirely shake off the regret which hangs over them that they are past joys which will not return.

Try as he may to find some hope with the help of friends, and even the clergyman of his parish, he knows that death is coming towards him as the grim reaper whose advance no power can halt. He may convince himself at times that 'death is not a thing to be feared'. But in his more realistic moments he knows that death will carry him away from all that he has ever known or experienced so far. He cannot pretend the change is either welcome or friendly.

Without a Bible to guide him he gropes his way as best he can, moving in the dark and edging every day closer to the darkness which is total and eternal. His friends, and even his minister, either do not or cannot tell him, that the Christless man is lost already in this life and is hastening with every passing hour, alas!, to a state of inconceivable misery and curse. This is the end of the ungodly man's life and, however much men scoff at hell, they cannot present one shred of proof to show that it is a false representation, or that the worldly man will not go there after death.

The death of a graceless man is an event of such tragic proportions that no words of man or angel could exaggerate its misery. Who, after all, can tell us here on earth what it means to lose one's soul (*Mark* 8:36)? Who can tell us what it means for a lost sinner to enter into the place where now he must pay for all his sins and yet have nothing with which to pay but an endless agony of tears? Let a man meet an angry lion rather than an angry God. But, if words mean what they say, the Bible makes it clear that the unconverted sinner, at his death, must enter into this worst of all possible states – that of 'eternal punishment' (*Matt.* 25:46).

Scarcely any mockery on earth is so great as that to be witnessed at some funerals of worldly persons. The greatest guilt for these is that of the officiating minister. The prayer is a eulogy of the deceased man or woman. The sermon is a rehearsal of the Judgment Day, in which the clergyman takes upon him the role of one who has power to declare that 'this our beloved brother/sister is now at peace'. Let the departed man be never so much a man of the world, the minister will 'put him into heaven'. Let a man be a heavy drinker, an atheist, a gambler, a lover of coarse pleasures, an unrepentant idolater – he is certain to be translated to glory at his funeral service by the pious prayers and laudations of some preachers. Well has it been said, If you want to hear a minister telling lies, go to a funeral service.

Where a man has lived a godly life, let this be stated at his funeral and let all who love his memory be assured that he is now indeed 'at rest'. But if there was no godly life, no faith in Christ, no final repentance, let nothing be said. A wise silence concerning the dead may convey a powerful message to the living who are still foolish. The funeral service is an occasion when the preacher should remind worldly people of their own need to prepare to meet God. At funerals we never affirm that a soul has gone to hell; but we must not state that a soul has gone to heaven if there was no evidence of grace, not even a little, in their life-time.

The only rest into which a Christless man enters at death is the fictitious rest invented by ignorant or cowardly clergymen who cannot, or dare not, confine their references about the recently deceased to what Scripture-light sanctions and allows. Those who live for this world and then at their last end employ at their funerals ministers who put them easily to heaven no doubt have their reward. They are at least in the minds of mourning relatives and friends, now decently buried and clerically qualified for the happy life of heaven. The funeral service over, the mourners retire from the grave-side to the warmth of an hotel and so back to the same worldly life as before. They are unwarned, uninstructed, unprepared for their own last end. All the tearful relatives part with a handshake and a kiss till the next family funeral. The overwhelmingly great and universal impression from the day's proceedings is that all go to heaven when they die and all are at rest.

There is more bad theology conveyed by such atrocious funeral services than many suppose. The implied false doctrines deserve to be listed for posterity: 'God pardons all men's sins regardless of the state of their souls.' 'Christ's death avails for those who never in this life believe in him.' 'All men are happy after death.' 'God does not care how we live on earth.' 'Courtesy to the bereaved means that we must not tell the truth about life after death.' 'It is better to let the ignorant go on in their ignorance than to upset them with any fear as to the future life.' 'A minister and a church-funeral put everything right in the end.' Far different is the death of the man who truly believes in Christ. Of him it is written that he shall 'rest from his labours' (*Rev.* 14:13). This man's rest is not imagined but real. His body, still united to Christ, rests in the grave as in a bed. His soul enters into the sublime rest of victory over all life's trials and troubles. 'He shall enter into peace' (*Isa.* 57:2). 'The end of that man is peace' (*Psa.* 37:37).

None but those who have experienced it can tell how sweet the feeling must be of having just entered into the saint's everlasting rest. Shall we speak of the bliss of looking up into the radiant face of a Saviour whom we have sought to serve a little here on earth and of receiving from his lips an affectionate 'Well done!'? Shall we refer to the immediate presence of the Triune God, that ultimate, transcendental Mystery whom all heaven shall eternally adore? Shall we mention the innumerable spirits of just men now 'made perfect' (*Heb.* 12:23) who are to be our companions and our fellow-servants for ever?

O the rest which God's people shall have when they are, one by one, called to 'come up higher' (*Luke* 14:10), to leave this lower theatre of war and to take their places with God's blessed dead on high! Here, all is watching, waiting, praying, fasting, hoping. But there, in Christ's near presence, all is to be resting, enjoying, adoring, feeling, partaking, drinking from the Fountain of life, which is Christ himself.

A great part of a Christian's life here below is to be on the outside of this world's 'good things'. The believer is excluded from so much that the world provides of pleasure and happiness. The polluted joys of sinners are no fit entertainment for Christ's people. We dare not sit down to their tempting morsels, nor sing their bawdy songs, nor dance to their tunes, nor clap at their jokes. The worldly man's laughter is like the 'crackling of thorns under a pot' (*Eccles.* 7:6). Half the places on earth are no-go areas for God's people. We go through those doors at our peril. The price of entry is death to the soul. Those professing Christians who are so unwise as to venture in will not come out again without sorrow and loss. Remember Samson and be warned!

But when the saint reaches his rest he will be welcome to enter where he may. No room in the saint's house-of-rest above has any lewdness or poison of sin in it. It is all holy, all innocent, all edifying, all sanctified, all glorious. The whole is luminous with the presence of God and of the Lamb. It is, in every part of it, his 'Father's house' (*John* 14:2) because it is Christ's 'Father's house'.

The Christian life can only get better and better. On earth it is good; after death to be with Christ is 'far better' (*Phil. 1:23*); after the resurrection of the last day it will be best of all. The saint's rest in death is not the end of his reward but only the first part of it. It is to be augmented still further when Christ bids the archangel to blow the last blast on his trumpet (*1 Thess.* 4:16; *1 Cor.* 15:52).

The rest of God's people in death is the prelude to their full, total and consummated joy when they receive their bodies back from the cold grave and wear them in their newly beautified condition, freshly brought up by Christ from the dust of death, all lustrous with sinlessness and bright glory. As surely as Christ rose from the grave, so certainly will he raise his own believing people up and marry them to himself forever: 'Thy Maker is thy husband' (*Isa.* 54:5).

More than two thousand years of time have passed. Time is hurrying on, till 'time shall be no longer' (*Rev.* 10:6). The saint's rest is nearer today than ever it was – not the sleep of death only, but the eternal state. Who knows but that even now the archangel is preparing to sound his trumpet? Happy and blessed are those who are then found doing their Master's will faithfully. He himself 'will come forth and serve them' (*Luke* 12:37).

27

Heaven, Resurrection, and the Coming Glory

It is common to refer to heaven as the place to which Christians go when they die. This is not entirely correct. The heavenly state of the Christian after death is not the full heaven which is to be revealed at the end of the world. It is for this full and final heaven that the believer longs, even more than for what he will enjoy after death. The souls of God's people who have died yearn too for the coming of the fully-restored heavens and earth. In glory the spirits of just men cry, 'How long, O Lord?' (*Rev.* 6:10). They too are not yet complete (*Heb.* 11:40). We generally refer to the glory into which Christians enter at death as the Intermediate State.

There is very much about a believer's death that differs from the death of an unbeliever. The Christian enters into a state of death as a thing prepared for him by God. It is a blessing to him. It is the gateway to glory. The Bible refers to this in such comforting terms as these: 'Blessed are the dead which die in the Lord from henceforth: Yea, saith the Spirit, that they may rest from their labours; and their works do follow them' (*Rev.* 14:13). When a Christian dies there are angels at hand to carry his soul into the nearer presence of God (*Luke* 16:22). It is a mark of honour and of favour. This event occurs at once and is evidently so rapid that 'to be absent from the body is to be present with the Lord' (*2 Cor.* 5:8). There is no period of 'purification' required, as some have taught. When the believer first trusted in Jesus he was fully cleansed by Christ's blood and justified from all his sins, whether original or actual, whether lesser (sometimes incorrectly termed 'venial') or greater (sometimes termed 'mortal') sins. 'The blood of Jesus Christ his Son cleanseth us from all sin' (*1 John* 1:7). The Christian dies a fully-pardoned man and is eligible for heaven at once, being clothed in the righteousness of the Lord Jesus Christ.

The unbeliever's death is very terrible. He dies under God's curse and displeasure. Death for him is death with the sting in it because he is laden with the guilt of his past life (*1 Cor.* 15:56). He enters into the Intermediate State of hell and realizes at once that he faces an eternity of misery. There is no 'second chance' of mercy after death. The only landmark on his dark and dismal horizon is the coming judgment day when his body will be raised 'in shame' from the grave. Reunited, soul and body together will at last be cast into the final state of hell (*Rev.* 20:15). No wonder Christ solemnly declares, 'There shall be weeping and gnashing of teeth' (*Matt.* 8:12)!

The state of the believer after death will be one of blessedness and yet also of imperfection. The believer's blessedness will consist in a number of things:

His soul will now be made entirely sanctified and holy. We could deduce this from the fact that he is allowed into the presence of God, where none but the entirely pure are allowed to dwell (*Psa.* 24:3, 4). However the Word of God informs us clearly that Christians at their death become 'the spirits of just men made perfect' (*Heb.* 12:23). The Book of Revelation portrays them as 'arrayed in white robes' (*Rev.* 7:13), white being the symbol of joy, victory and purity. They 'came out of great tribulation, and have washed their robes, and made them white in the blood of the Lamb' (*Rev.* 7:14). The 'tribulation' here is the suffering and persecution which they have gone through on earth. This verse speaks of the souls of all believers after death. It does not refer to some special category of saints who are to go through a future period of history called 'the tribulation', a view wrongly held by many Christians influenced by dispensationalism.

The believer will be 'with Christ which is far better' (*Phil.* 1:23). This state is far better for the believer than life on earth ever was, even at its best. His soul will be in sight of the throne of God and he will see the Saviour and worship him. In this respect the souls of believers in the New Testament age are more privileged than in Old Testament times, since the Son of God was then not yet incarnate and so not yet visible to the saints in glory as now he is.

It must have been a most glorious and majestic spectacle for the blessed dead to see the Son of God take his seat on the throne of heaven after he had completed his ministry upon earth. In that hour they saw the fulfilment of the Psalm: 'Lift up your heads, O ye gates; and be ye lift up, ye everlasting doors; and the King of glory shall come in. Who is this King of glory? The Lord strong and mighty, the Lord mighty in battle. Lift up your heads, O ye gates; even lift them up, ye everlasting doors; and the King of glory shall come in. Who is this King of glory? The Lord of hosts, he is the King of glory' (*Psa.* 24:7–10).

It must also be a sublime privilege for them now to gaze upon the 'Lamb in the midst of the throne' (*Rev.* 5:6). At this glorious sight the redeemed join in ecstatic praises as they sing: 'Worthy is the Lamb that was slain to receive power, and riches, and wisdom, and strength and honour, and glory, and blessing' (*Rev.* 5:12). And as they do so, the whole upper world re-echoes their song with the cry: 'Blessing and honour, and glory, and power, be unto him that sitteth upon the throne, and unto the Lamb for ever and ever' (*Rev.* 5:13). To this, the four celestial living creatures add their angelic 'Amen!' (*Rev.* 5:14).

There are many wonderful aspects to Christ's ministry in heaven now and these are visible to the saints in their blessed state after death. The spirits in glory look upon their Saviour with the most rapt attention. They appreciate his work for them with unspeakably great gratitude, love and worship: 'Unto him that loved us, and washed us from our sins in his own blood, and hath made us kings and priests unto God and his Father; to him be glory and dominion for ever and ever' (*Rev.* 1:5–6).

They are now beyond all trouble and enjoy the personal affection for them of the Lord Jesus Christ himself. In Revelation 7:15–17 we are given a picture of these aspects of their present joy and comfort in the following exquisite words: 'Therefore are they before the throne of God, and serve him day and night in his temple: and he that sitteth on the throne shall dwell among them. They shall hunger no more, neither thirst any more; neither shall the sun light on them, nor any heat. For the Lamb which is in the midst of the throne shall feed them, and shall lead them unto living fountains of waters: and God shall wipe away all tears from their eyes.'

After death the souls of believers enjoy the close, abiding and reassuring presence of God and of Christ. They are not inactive but are engaged in delightful service to the God whom they love. They are beyond the reach of all trouble and sorrow. God will compensate and comfort them for all their sufferings upon earth. Christ will satisfy them and bless them in every way.

The Bible makes it clear however that the believer is incomplete in this Intermediate State between death and the resurrection. One of the fullest passages on this aspect of our theme is this: 'For we know that if our earthly house of this tabernacle were dissolved, we have a building of God, an house not made with hands, eternal in the heavens. For in this we groan, earnestly desiring to be clothed upon with our house which is from heaven: If so be that being clothed we shall not be found naked. For we that are in this taber-nacle do groan, being burdened: not for that we would be unclothed, but clothed upon, that mortality might be swal-lowed up of life' (*2 Cor.* 5:1–4).

Paul here compares the body to a tent or tabernacle. He envisages that the body, or 'tent', in which the believer now lives on earth will be destroyed by death. In that case, the believer will be 'absent from the body and present with the Lord'. In that condition he will be 'naked' or 'unclothed'.

But the Christian will receive a 'house' to live in at the day of resurrection. This new home will be much superior to the present one in that it will last forever and will be perfectly suited to the heavenly state. When we receive that body we shall be in a state in which 'mortality is swallowed up of life'. In the present body 'we groan and are burdened' because of its frailty and mortality. We long for the resurrection condition. But we are content, if need be, to be 'unclothed' for a time. Death for the Christian is better than life; but the resurrection-state is better still.

Paul evidently envisages three conditions of a believer: (1) the present life during which we are in this weak and frail body; (2) the state after death in which we are naked and unclothed; (3) the future state after the resurrection, when we shall receive a glorious body.

Paul also explains to us what our attitude should be in the light of these three conditions. 'We groan and are burdened' in this present life. We long for the state in which we are to be at Christ's return, when we shall be clothed with the body of glory. Christians who survive in this life till Christ's return will come to this state without seeing death. Many believers will long since have died when the Second Coming occurs. Even so, we are content as Christians to fall 'asleep in Jesus' and so to become disembodied for a period of time. Our present groanings and yearnings are God-given. They are indited by the Holy Spirit in our hearts and are an anticipation of our coming glory.

Death is good for a Christian because it will usher him into the presence of Christ. But that is an incomplete state. The believer's ultimate goal is to have a body of glory. Till that is given to him he will be incomplete, even in the heaven-after-death condition. But all believers will come to the final state of resurrection unto life at last.

A thoughtful person is bound to have questions about the condition of Christians after death. Will Christians know one another after death? Is there any knowledge of earthly things by the souls of believers in glory? We look at these two questions in concluding our short study.

1. *Will Christians know one another after death?*

There are good reasons for believing that Christians will certainly know one another after death. This is suggested by the very consideration that the believer's state after death will be a better one than the present. Though the soul is disembodied it does not lose its identity. 'God is not the God of the dead but of the living', said Christ (*Matt.* 22:32). It is one characteristic of those who live that they have powers of recognition and the memory of past friends.

It would seem inconceivable that believers will live in ignorance of one another's identity till the end of the world. It is true that they are, above all 'with Christ'. No doubt this one fact alone is sufficiently comforting. Hebrews 12:22–24 leads us to believe we shall have knowledge of one another. 'But ye are come unto mount Sion, and unto the city of the living God, the heavenly Jerusalem, and to an innumerable company of angels; to the general assembly and church of the firstborn, which are written in heaven, and to God the Judge of all, and to the spirits of just men made perfect, and to Jesus the mediator of the new covenant, and to the blood of sprinkling, that speaketh better things than that of Abel.'

Such terms here as 'general assembly' and 'church of the firstborn' suggest a gathering of God's people above which has a mutually-familiar society. How 'the spirits of just men made perfect' could be said to form an 'assembly' or 'church' and yet not know one another's identity surpasses all comprehension. It seems most probable that the phrase 'written in heaven', implies that all are known by name to the entire redeemed company.

2. *Do the souls of the redeemed know about what happens on earth?*

This is an intriguing question and one which is not easy to answer.

It is about as much as we know from Scripture to make the following points. The redeemed in glory know at least as much about God's future purposes as we now know of them from the Bible. It is likely that they know considerably more since they are in the direct presence of God himself, the Author of all revelation. Further, the redeemed are in the presence of the angels who are said to rejoice at the conversion of sinners on earth (*Luke* 15:7, 10). When Christ says that 'joy shall be in heaven over one sinner that repenteth' it may imply that the redeemed, as well as the angels are informed whenever sinners on earth are converted. It seems difficult to see how the angels could rejoice in heaven and the spirits of the redeemed not know that they rejoice at the conversion of men.

But we dare not go beyond what God has said in his Word. Let us press on towards heaven that we may know the things now hidden from us – and so be blessed in and with our Saviour Jesus Christ forever!

28

'As the Lightning . . .'

Nothing ought to matter to us in this life like the getting safely out of it. If we do *that*, we shall do what is of most importance, even though we shall have done little or nothing here of importance in the eyes of worldly men. On the other hand, we shall have squandered life utterly and eternally if we succeed in everything except our safe departure to a better world. Grace, when it enters the soul of a man at his conversion, teaches him that 'one thing is needful' and that he had better lose all he has rather than 'lose his own soul'. Grace in the soul gives it a holy urgency to prepare for the end of all things as they are now in this present temporary state. The effect of conversion is to throw the centre of gravity of our thoughts forward from the present to that last great end-time of the world.

Our Saviour has portrayed the end-time of this world in such vivid and awesome language that all these instincts of grace within us are quickened with a tenfold urgency. To be ready for the great Day of the Lord when it comes is clearly *the* clarion call of Christ to us. He and his inspired prophets and apostles depict the end of the world in language which might well make the very angels to shudder, lest even they, if it were possible, should be unprepared for it.

The history of our little world is not unlike some great symphony composed by a master musician. It has its themes and counter-themes. It has its moments of drama and its passages of calm. It has its movements and its overall progression. But above all else, it will have its terrible finale, a finale more dramatic, more conclusive and more final than the greatest genius of man could ever imagine or devise.

The end of history is to be no less an experience than for us all to encounter God himself. When the drama is over and the curtain finally falls on the stage of human affairs, the actors and the audience are both alike to make the acquaintance of the divine Dramatist in person. The One who has throughout history hidden himself so largely in the background will then, in that last Great Day, finally appear to take the centre stage. Every eye will be upon him alone, and every thought will be swallowed up in the universal collective realization that nothing at all matters like having his favour and not his frown. If men had not had that realization before, they will certainly have it in that solemn hour. God will be all that matters then.

'As the lightning cometh out of the east, and shineth even unto the west, so shall also the coming of the Son of man be' (*Matt.* 24:27). No normal creature – whether man or beast – loves lightning. It sends strong men to their knees. It reduces wild beasts to silent fear. The atheist himself is ready to pray when he is confronted with lightning. We know instinctively that it is a formidable and a deadly power. The heathen who are in other respects so blind in their ideas of God, are at least right to ascribe to lightning a heavenly and divine source. Only fools laugh at lightning. There will be no laughter of fools when that event takes place which Christ describes as like 'the lightning'.

The last day is an event which Jesus Christ prophesies will be heralded by a vast global streak of lightning, visible from pole to pole of this universe. The Second Coming of Jesus will be the rudest shock ever felt by mankind. If the Flood of Noah's day was dreadful, the Second Coming will be a thousand times more dreadful. If the cataracts of fire which fell on Sodom and Gomorrah were dire, the final coming of Christ will, for the wicked, be dire in the extreme. No atomic or other explosion made by the hand of man will inspire such awe or command such universal silence as this appearing of the Son of man upon the clouds of heaven. It is the terminal knell of God, and it will summon us all either to heaven or to hell.

It is good for the Christian to pause regularly in the busy course of life in order to remind himself of this text of our Lord and Saviour: 'As the *lightning* . . . so shall . . . the coming of the Son of man be' (*Matt.* 24:27). It is a text fitted to recall the believer to sanity in this tragic and perverse generation. Never (or perhaps seldom) has mankind been so fast asleep to divine judgment as it is today. Our age is giddy with endless trivial pleasures and pursuits.

Rare are the voices raised today to recall men's minds and consciences to the stark realities of death, judgment and eternity! Sermons there are in plenty which soothe and caress the hearers into careless ease and carnal security. 'Peace, peace' is heard on every side. But our careless age needs to be wakened up and reminded of the thunder-storm which is to put an end to all mankind's soft and lawless pleasures in the end. What a tonic it would be to hear at least some radio preachers summon up the courage to warn their hearers of the coming thunder-bolt and lightning-flash!

Not the least serious side to the Saviour's prediction that his Second Coming will be like the lightning is the fact that we do not know *when* it will take place. If sinners were able to calculate 'the day and the hour', as they are able to calculate the weight of the earth or the speed of light, they might relax till a short space before the great event itself. If they knew just *when* our Lord's return were to occur, men might, with some appearance of reason, continue in their reckless pursuit of vain pleasure till the eve of the coming divine holocaust. If men knew *when* the lightning was to strike, they could program their computers to serve notice on the world that the eleventh hour had arrived and men must now prepare to meet their God.

The fact that God has told us of the lightning-day but not the date of it, however, is evidence enough that we had better 'watch and pray' now and every day, in case that Day should come on us unawares and find us unprepared. The worldly man's gamble with life's pleasures and his heedless disregard of the coming lightning-storm is as suicidal as the game of Russian roulette. The next sin that men commit may be their last.

A man who knows that a tornado is about to strike his house lives very differently from another man who is ignorant of the warning signs in the weather. This is the difference between the believer and the man of the world. The believer, like Noah, is 'moved with fear' (*Heb.* 11:7) every day he lives. The believer is, in a manner of speaking, always in a hurry in this life. His agenda is to get safely through this world and safely out of it. He handles the world with care. His concern is to use the world so as not to abuse it. The believer's eyes are not simply on the world before him. He lives with one eye on the heavens. He looks up and knows that his redemption is drawing nearer with each passing day and hour. He is aware that the lightning-flash is still to come.

Oh, what a day that will be when Christ is seen in the heavens in all his glory! What a sight that will be when the heavens and earth shall flee away in a moment to expose at last the glorious throne of God, a throne of perfect and inflexible righteousness! God forbid that we should ever forget the coming great Day when seas will evaporate, stars collapse, mountains be removed and the present universe sink in one gigantic meltdown of the elements! As when a huge liner is sinking in the ocean and every man for himself hunts for some way of escape, so shall the end of this world be.

When the lightning flashes from east to west and bleak eternity stares mankind in the face, the air will be rent with the cries and groans of many billions of unprepared souls. Would God that we might, as Christians, be stirred to do all we can now, before the fatal lightning flashes, to have the one true gospel made known to sinners far and wide in every land and every language! Once the midnight hour strikes, this gospel age will close for ever and the filthy will be 'filthy still' (*Rev.* 22:11) with a filthiness in which poor lost sinners will wallow for a million, million ages of misery.

The lightning-like arrival of Jesus Christ will be the end of all sorrow to those who love him. Like a flock of birds the elect will rise up on the wing to greet him with songs of joy and adoration. They will meet him 'in the air' (*1 Thess.* 4:17). It is the reunion of friends who meet to part no more. The final separation between the righteous and the wicked now takes place, 'the one shall be taken and the other left' (*Matt.* 24:40).

The magnetism of God's electing love will find out every one of those on earth whose names are in the Book of Life. With infallible certainty every last one of them – and even the very least of them – will be lifted up from the earth to gather around their Saviour in his majesty and glory as he sits on the clouds above. They are the welcoming party who cry, 'Lo, this is our God; we have waited for him!' (*Isa.* 25:9). The sea will give up its dead and death and hell will give up their dead.

For all who meekly serve Jesus now in this life, death will be over and done forever when he comes to reign. The lightning-flash of his Second Coming will be the harbinger of their full and perfect glorification. For them, now death shall be swallowed up by life and mortality by immortality. They will be now ushered into the everlasting Kingdom of light and love with Christ eternally. Oh, blessed prospect!

When Christ comes like the lightning, all a believer's present cares will end abruptly. Our light affliction is then over. With divine lavishness he will make much then of our little acts of service to his Great Name. Did we preach a little for him? He will reward it with ten thousand-fold honours of kind appreciation. Did we live a little for him and speak well of him here below? He will not forget such faithfulness when he comes at last. A cup of cold water given in the name of a disciple will receive its ample reward from him.

If this sad age is bent on forgetting all that our Lord Jesus has said about the coming great Day of God, let believers call it to mind all the more frequently. The more careless the world grows, the more careful God's children need to be. Even now, for all that we know, the archangel is putting to his lips that golden trumpet whose awful last blast will summon the living and the dead before the tribunal of Almighty God. In spite of all this world's ridicule and scorn, one thing is certain: Christ is coming to judge the world. And his coming will be like the lightning.

29

From Prophecy to History

Prophecy and history are the same thing looked at from different points of view. Prophecy is history not yet fulfilled; history is prophecy now fulfilled. The march of time means inevitably that less and less prophecy requires to be fulfilled. The purpose of God, conceived in eternity past, is daily enacted before our eyes. The things which the Scriptures long ago foretold are becoming realities which every man can see. 'History' is therefore the word which we give to that part of God's decree which has now become realized in this world. 'Prophecy' is that remainder of God's purpose which will be realized in its time.

The manner in which the Bible presents to us both history and prophecy is entirely different from the manner in which this unbelieving world presents it. The Bible makes it clear that the progress of events in this world is neither haphazard nor fortuitous but according to an eternal purpose. God, in other words, has a plan for this world which he is slowly but surely bringing to pass. A divine, yet unseen, hand is infallibly guiding all the affairs of men and nations. The sudden eruptions of war and calamity, the sudden collapse of governments and empires, are all events which God himself has purposed from eternity past and which he is making effectual in the course of time.

In the biblical view of life there is no place for fortuitous events, or events that have no cause. All events have a cause, and all events have a meaning. We may not yet understand why certain events take place and we may not yet be in a position to assign a reason for their occurrence. But we must never leave room in our thinking for meaningless events. Our proper attitude to all events is to recognize that they are of divine origin and contribute in one way or another towards the fulfilment of God's wise purpose.

Even the worst crimes committed by evil men are to be interpreted always as having their origin in God's plan and as contributing to its outworking. There is undoubted mystery in the way God's plan relates to criminal actions. But we must not interpret any events, even the worst events, as if they were somehow outside the sphere of God's control or purpose. To do so is latent atheism and will lead to a state of despair and hopelessness. Up to a point we can understand the relationship between God's plan and men's criminal actions. We correctly say that God 'permits' sinful actions. By that we mean that God allows evil men on occasion to commit atrociously evil actions but that he at the same time disapproves of the evil of these actions. In all such crimes we can see that God disapproves of the wicked motive but wills to permit the action for wise and good ends. There are numerous cases of this in history. The supreme example is the crucifixion of Christ. No crime could be greater; yet God had ordained the crucifixion in order to save the world. What men did, for evil, God meant for good. In all crimes, God disapproves the evil motives of men but permits their evil actions for a good reason.

A great many of the prophecies of God's Word are brought to their fulfilment by the evil actions of men. All unknown to sinful men, God has permitted their evil actions to be a part of his unseen plan to do good to the world. Thus, Pharoah's refusal to let Israel go out of Egypt was a major factor in God's plan to deliver his people from their long bondage and give them a land of their own, according to promise.

Part of our confusion arises, when we study this subject, from a failure to define what we mean by God's 'will'. We may ask the question: Was it God's will that Pharoah should harden his heart and refuse to let Israel go – at least, at first, until the ten plagues overwhelmed both him and all the Egyptians? The answer we give revolves round the precise sense in which we use the world 'will' here.

To clarify the sense in which we use the term 'will' of God, we must see that there are two senses in which God may be said to 'will' any event. There is a sense in which God wills only what is agreeable to his own holy nature. This is his will of approbation, or approval. God cannot will with approval any action which is in itself sinful.

On the other hand, we may use the same word 'will' of God in the sense of his secret purpose or decree. In this sense we may say that God 'wills' all events, even the very wickedest and worst. However when we say that God 'wills' sinful events we mean that he permits, and indeed ordains, them in his purpose but does not by any means approve the sinfulness of them. For example, God 'willed' that Judas should betray Christ in that the event had been eternally decreed by God and was the subject of several Old Testament prophecies (see Psalms 41, 55, 109; Zechariah 11). But we in no sense here mean that God approved of Judas' treason.

The practical benefit of grasping this distinction in the use of the word 'will' in reference to God is that we must always take the Moral Law of the Bible as our rule of action. To obey the Moral Law is always pleasing to God. It is our clear rule of life. However, God's secret purpose mysteriously makes use of the sins of men, which, though in themselves hateful to God, are nevertheless wisely overruled by him for good. Secret things belong to God; but our duty is to do what he has revealed and commanded (*Deut.* 29:29).

One of the most impressive things about the Bible's presentation of history and prophecy is its deep seriousness. There is never a light-heartedness in the way the Bible looks back or else looks forward. History and prophecy are not light or trivial things but matters of great moment. When the Bible looks back in time it speaks with a voice of admonition: 'Remember the Flood.' 'Remember Sodom and the fire that fell.' 'Remember what happened to Egypt at the Exodus.' 'Remember lessons from the days of the Judges – from the apostasy of Israel – from the pride of Babylon – from the haughtiness of Edom and the other pagan nations.' 'Remember the fall of the Jews at their rejection of the Messiah.'

This emphasis is found all through the Bible wherever it refers back to past events. The biblical view of history is not simply that history is academically interesting, or fascinating – but that it is fraught with lessons for us to learn from today. The reason for this is that behind history stands God himself. God's use of history is therefore magisterial. He uses it to teach us vitally important lessons for our lives today. God's presentation of history in the Bible should put us into a mood of serious recognition that it is a terrible thing to offend him by pride, by rebellion or by unbelief.

Similarly, the Bible's presentation of prophecy is always characterized by deep seriousness. Whatever divergent views we may have about prophecy, there is no dispute on one point: Bible prophecies are extremely serious things. Even a cursory reading of the Book of Revelation shows that it views future events in an awesomely grave light: trumpets blown by angels warn mankind; vials of wrath are poured out on this world; beastly figures of indescribable cruelty fight against God's people; a lake of fire at last receives the body and soul of every wicked man. In every sense, these prophecies are 'apocalyptic'. They are given to instil reverence for God, fear of offending him, and a profound sense of urgency in every one who reads this great final book of the Bible.

Not the least of the benefits which we have by reading and studying the Bible is that we gain a total view of all that is to happen in this world. The man who ignores his Bible sees at best only that part of the plan which lies in the past. He knows nothing of the great events still future, which form the theme of biblical prophecies. He cannot see the whole picture. But the believing and devout Bible student sees the entire picture – at least in outline.

The Bible-student sees all events in a framework which both satisfies his mind and quietens his fears. He sees that God is over all events, even the worst. He sees that whatever is happening now, whether it be wars or calamities, will issue some day in good to all those who love God. As the current of the river carries the boats downstream, so God's providence is carrying all events towards their goal, a goal which will spell everlasting blessing to those who are God's children. The blessings which are locked up for us in the prophecies will, by and by, be solid joys for us when the time to show them openly is come.

When the last trumpet sounds, all the prophecies will have become history and time will be no longer. Then God's purpose will have reached its zenith; God will be all in all to all his people, saved by Christ and sanctified by the Spirit.

When we hear the noise of war and the alarm of battle, our hearts bleed with sorrow for those who are afflicted. But we know from Scripture that all current events, like the wheels of a great clock, are moving towards the midnight cry: 'Behold, the Bridegroom cometh!'

30

'Thy Kingdom Come'

One fundamental difference between the Christian's life and that of the unbeliever is their respective attitudes to the world to come. The unbeliever instinctively shrinks from all thought of what lies beyond this life. If he thinks of it at all, as at times he must, he is glad to turn away from the subject to find comfort in present things which are familiar to him: home, family, work and, especially, pleasure and happiness. The unbeliever's philosophy has always been *carpe diem* ('enjoy life now while you have it') and leave discussion about the shadowy and uncertain things of a future world to sages and sour philosophers. That was the typical outlook of the ancient pagans whose writings have come down to us, and it is the typical outlook of the modern pagans whose songs we can hear sung any hour of the day.

This reluctance in the unbeliever to dwell long on a future life is understandable. He has little joy at the thought of leaving this present life, and he has no good grounds for thinking that any future life, if future life there be, will prove half so good as this one. In moments of fleeting piety, perhaps at a funeral or beside a sick-bed, he can bring himself to speak respectfully of 'heaven', 'peace' and 'eternal rest'. But he knows at heart that he would far rather keep this present troubled life than have any future one, however 'peaceful'.

Just why the unbeliever is so unenthusiastic for the life to come is all too plain to see. He is in love with this present world. His heart is wrapped around its fleeting pleasures. His roots are all sunk in earth's present comforts, however imperfect they are. The very word 'hope' means for him nothing higher than to get more of *this* world's good: more of its 'fun', more 'luck' in placing his bet on a winning horse or a winning team, a larger mouthful from the world's blissful cup of laughter and smiling mirth.

The worldly man's 'hope' is not of good beyond the grave but good before it. His sights are set not on enjoying a fair land beyond this life, but on this life alone, and as long as he can, on clinging fast to it. His ambitions are carnal to the core, even when he may have had some smatterings of religion mixed with them; as a churchman once betrayed, when, at his retirement, he said: 'I have spent the last forty years pleasing God, and now I intend to please myself!'

The worldly man's view of heaven is to enjoy the pleasures of sin without interruption. For him, everything to do with religion only gets in the way of what he really wants. Like Cain, he worships God, if ever, only with his second-best. The language of his heart is: 'Woe betide anyone who comes between me and my happiness! He who preaches to me of life after death only spoils my present heaven here on earth!'

What are half the wars of history, but only so many angry protests of worldly men against the biblical view that the spiritual is above the natural and the heavenly life better than this earthly one? Earth's mighty men have, like Nimrod their father, striven to build their Babylons here below. Whenever God has broken down their works, as he did at the Flood, at the Tower of Babel and at countless times since, it has been in order to serve notice on mankind that he will in the end throw down all this world to bring in a better. But the Caesars, the Herods, the Napoleons, and the Hitlers have never been able to read this great lesson of history. Christless eyes see no kingdoms but of this world; and Christless rulers, like Pilate, suppose it to be a joke when they hear of a kingdom which is 'not of this world' (*John* 18:36).

What Christless eyes do not see, however, is what Christian men and women of all ages have deeply hoped for and believed in. They have done so when they have taken the Lord's Supper and 'shown forth the Lord's death *till he come*' (*1 Cor.* 11:26). They have done so in their Creed: 'I believe in . . . the life everlasting'. They have done so when they have buried their blessed dead out of their sight 'in sure and certain hope of life everlasting'. The Christian's hope, even on the admission of an apostle, is nothing if it is a this-worldly hope and nothing more: 'If in this life only we have hope in Christ, we are of all men most miserable' (*1 Cor.* 15:19). But it is infinitely more. The Christian's hope is the solid and certain confidence of seeing *God* at last.

While the worldly man lives for this life, the believer lives for the life beyond this life. The believer's life is hid in God and is intertwined with Christ in all that he is. Religious conversion is both a crucifixion and a resurrection to a new life. At his conversion a believer dies to this world, is crucified to it, is taken out of it into a state of mortification to earthly things. His soul is knit to Christ in love. *Christ* is his righteousness, his ambition, his 'exceeding great reward'. He has been raised with Christ to a hope which is fed by mysterious streams of grace within him and which teach him daily to look for 'a better country, that is an heavenly' (*Heb.* 11:16). The current of a believer's hope is stronger than all earthly instincts. He is prepared to lose all the world that in the end he may gain Christ and so enjoy him forever.

The call of God within the believer's soul is a powerful but mysterious voice. Even the Apostle Paul, who had gone into the 'third heaven', must admit that in this life 'we see through a glass darkly' (*1 Cor.*13:12). The Spirit assures us by his Word and by his inward influence that the kingdom to which we travel is a most excellent place. But how we are persuaded so completely of something we have not yet seen cannot be explained to any who have not heard God's voice in their own hearts. The believer, however, is utterly convinced of the reality of heaven, and he is prepared 'with patience' to 'wait for it' (*Rom.* 8:25).

'Thy kingdom come.' How many mouths have uttered this famous prayer since our Lord taught it to his disciples! It is a prayer which daily draws nearer to fulfilment. Like all true prayers, it is prophetic. The kingdom of Christ is nearer now than ever it was. Soon the trumpet of Jubilee will sound and the King will return to usher all true believers into their eternal state of glory! They will come from the north and from the south, from the east and from the west to 'sit down with Abraham, Isaac and Jacob in the kingdom of heaven' (*Matt.* 8:11). All the Scriptures harmonize with this clear message: The Lord is coming soon!

Much as we have enjoyed feeding on Christ by faith in this life, we shall have vastly greater measures of this joy in us when his kingdom comes at last. Oh, what mysteries we shall have to satisfy our minds in that consummated state: the mystery of the Triune God, the mystery of the incarnate Lord, the mystery of our union with him and with all his! What secrets will be unveiled then for us to see 'face to face' (*1 Cor.* 13:12): the perfect wisdom of God's eternal decree, the perfect wisdom of his providence, the perfect wisdom of his way with every saint and every sinner!

The kingdom to which we are travelling will not be like the kingdoms we have known here on earth. All its inhabitants will be holy, faithful and good. They will all have a fair record of service to their King while they were here on earth. They will be filled with love to Christ and to one another. The kingdom which is coming soon will know neither the slightest stain of sin nor the slightest whisper of Satan. No funerals will be held. No inhabitant shall ever say, 'I am sick.' None shall hunger there and none shall thirst. The cry of pain will not be heard in that place, nor the din of battle, but all her inhabitants will sing for joy. They will *see* God. They will be near him and be blessed by him in every way, so that all the sorrows of this present life will be forgotten and all the sins of this present life forgiven forever.

If the Christian has enemies, no wonder they scheme day and night to stop him from entering so great a kingdom or enjoying such a full cup of God's love! However little non-Christians may believe in this heavenly kingdom, Satan and all the demons of hell believe it very well. If they did not, they would not be at such pains to deceive the wicked or to hinder our progress to this great kingdom above.

One evidence that heaven is a real place is that Satan works so hard to have men think it unreal. To the man in the street, heaven is just 'pie in the sky when you die'. To the clever scholar, no real heaven exists, but only 'realized eschatology'. Heaven is no more real than fairy-land. To the stern statesman, it is just so much 'opium of the people' to keep the masses happy.

To the Christian, heaven is a glorious reality where Christ, who is our hope, is already gone and where he waits for his own to join him – you, and even me.